'WOMEN WITH THE GOOD NEWS'
THE RHETORICAL HERITAGE OF PENTECOSTAL
HOLINESS WOMEN PREACHERS

'WOMEN WITH THE GOOD NEWS'

THE RHETORICAL HERITAGE OF PENTECOSTAL HOLINESS WOMEN PREACHERS

KRISTEN DAYLE WELCH

CPT

CPT Press
Cleveland, Tennessee

'Women with the Good News'
The Rhetorical Heritage of Pentecostal Holiness Women Preachers

Published by CPT Press
900 Walker ST NE
Cleveland, TN 37311
USA
email: cptpress@pentecostaltheology.org
website: www.pentecostaltheology.org

Library of Congress Control Number: 2010929463

ISBN-10: 0981965199
ISBN-13: 9780981965192

All quotations from the Bible are taken from Suggs, M. Jack, Katherine Doob Sakenfeld, and James R. Mueller (eds.), *The Oxford Study Bible: Revised English Bible With the Apocrypha: A Complete Guide to the World of the Bible* (New York: Oxford University Press, 1992).

The Lord speaks the word;
The women with the good news are a mighty host.
(Ps. 68.11, REB)

Dedicated to my family, my mentors, and my friends
'Success is not measured by the amount of status one attains;
it is measured by the degree to which one serves'.

CONTENTS

Acknowledgements

I would like sincerely to thank Dr. Theresa Enos for her guidance on my dissertation and on drafts of articles that became chapters in this book. Her continued support for my work has lent me the confidence I needed in order to continue my scholarship in this field. I would like to thank Dr. Harold Hunter for reading and commenting on parts of this book, for his support of my voice as a scholar in the IPHC denomination, and for his continued support of my work. I wish to also offer thanks to the CPT editors, Drs. Lee Roy Martin and John Christopher Thomas for the tireless work they have done editing this manuscript. No detail has been ignored and because of their efforts, this manuscript was greatly improved. Thanks also to Dr. Vinson Synan who served on my dissertation committee and helped lend my work veracity early on, and for Dr. Brian Jackson who carefully read and commented on an article that was partially revised and incorporated into this book.

I would also like to thank my mother, who has tirelessly helped me to read, edit, and revise this manuscript while also providing needed information for some of the current statistics on women in the IPHC. She is endlessly kind and patient. Her wisdom has been a source of strength for me all of my life.

Thanks also to the men and women I interviewed, to my friends and family who kept believing in me year after year as I drafted this material, and to my colleagues at Longwood University who encouraged me over the last three years as I struggled to teach and to write.

I have to especially thank my husband. He has never quit believing I could be successful in this field even though I have received many rejection letters along the way. He has seen every up and every down and still remained an ardent supporter of me as a wife, mother, teacher, and scholar.

Finally, thank you Grandma and Grandpa Scott for living lives of joy and hard work in a true spirit of Christianity. It was because of you that I have such a great dad, and it was because of you that my father's Christian character has set a standard not many can attain. I know full well that growing up in a good family is a rare treasure, and I know that only those who are familiar with what good character consists of can see it clearly manifested in the lives of others. Your investment in my father and my father's investment in me have helped me tremendously as I've written about IPHC preachers who lived lives of determination and self-sacrifice.

And thank you Grandma and Grandpa Rex. I know that my grandpa's life was well spent for the good of the IPHC and for the good of the souls he led to Christ during his ministry. He treasured this denomination and its people, and he passionately lived out the calling on his life. Grandma's strong support of him and our family made all of the difference. As a true prayer warrior, the work of her life was to love others, as she once told me. Thank you, Grandma.

Kristen Dayle Welch

INTRODUCTION

Any real attempt to address rhetoric, gender, and religion in the American Southwest ends up becoming a monumental task, worthy of more time and attention than it will be possible for me to give. I am aware that the title of this book might spark the interest of theologians, historians, social scientists, and, of course, scholars of rhetoric like me, so it is important to address the scope of my work in this introduction. Rhetoric, gender, and religion are broad terms and serve as a starting place for drawing out the specific aspects of ethos-making that I studied in the lives and contexts of the International Pentecostal Holiness Church's (IPHC) women preachers in Oklahoma that I have been studying and writing about since 2003. A look at 'what's missing' in this introduction will sharpen the lens of analysis employed in the remainder of the book.

What's Missing: Race

What has most noticeably been left out of this book is a discussion of race. It can hardly be ignored that the racial equality begun in the Azusa Street revivals of 1906-1908 dramatically changed the attitude of many influential early Pentecostals from one of prejudice to one of acceptance.[1] The example of the IPHC's change in attitude can be construed as somewhat representative of the changes experienced by other existing and emerging Pentecostal denominations, although numerous denominations arose or changed theological course as a result of these revivals.

In 1906, in response to mounting curiosity about the spirit baptism experiences being described on Azusa Street in Los Angeles, California, IPHC leader G.B. Cashwell traveled all the way across

---

[1] According to Pentecostal historian and theologian Harold D. Hunter, the Fire-Baptized was racially integrated prior to Azusa Street but split again in 1908 (Personal correspondence, May 26, 2010).

the United States by train to see what was happening for himself.[2] He was not prepared for what he saw and felt when he arrived. Historian Vinson Synan tells us that 'A great power could be felt several blocks from the building' where the revivals were held, and Cashwell arrived to see a mix of blacks and whites worshipping together. He entered, but it was 'unsettling' to him to see that the man in charge was African American William Seymour. It required five days of prayer for Cashwell to overcome his prejudice, but when he did Seymour was one of those who laid hands on him to pray for him to receive the baptism in the Holy Spirit. The experience was so life-changing, Cashwell hurried back to Dunn, North Carolina, and 'issued special invitations to all the ministers of the Holiness Church, the Fire-Baptized Holiness Church, and the holiness element of the Free-Will Baptist church' to come to hear him talk about the baptism of the Holy Spirit on December 31, 1906.[3] 'Hundreds' came and a one-month revival was begun that changed the practice of religion across the area.

Most Pentecostal denominations owe much to the ministry of William Seymour. The 'son of former slaves', Seymour was born in Centerville, Louisiana, in 1870.[4] He was described as a man of 'uncommon spiritual hunger' and is quoted as saying 'Such hunger to have more of God was in my heart ... that I prayed five hours a day for two and a half years'. Seymour refused to be bitter when he was made to learn from white preacher Charles Parham from out in the hallway instead of being given a chair in a class with whites. Blind in one eye and selflessly devoted to Christ, it seems his power came from his humility, not his pride.

In my opinion, it is clear that Seymour's success can be interpreted as evidence of God's displeasure with racism. After all, while white woman Agnes Ozman received the baptism of the Holy Spirit on January 1, 1901 when Parham prayed for her, neither Parham nor Ozman were able to change the current of American religion as Seymour did.[5] The ramifications of their experience went

---

[2] Vinson Synan, *The Old-Time Power: A History of the Pentecostal Holiness Church* (Franklin Springs, GA: Advocate Press, 1973), p. 107.

[3] Synan, *The Old-Time Power*, pp. 108-109.

[4] Eddie Hyatt, *The Azusa Street Revival: The Holy Spirit in America, 100 Years, Special Centennial Edition* (Lake Mary, FL: Strang Communications, 2006), p. 13.

[5] Vinson Synan, The *Century of the Holy Spirit: 100 Years of Pentecostal and Charismatic Renewal 1901-2001* (Nashville: Thomas Nelson, 2001), p. 1.

largely unnoticed, but Seymour's impact on American religion cannot be overstated.[6]

While issues of race have not had a problem-free, linear progression in the right direction in the IPHC's history or in the history of other Pentecostal denominations, in comparison to the rest of American society whose hearts were little changed until the work of Martin Luther King, Jr. in the 60s, Pentecostals were way ahead in the fight for racial equality.[7] Including the stories of anti-racism within the denominational histories of Pentecostal strands would provide a richer story of America's relationship with faith and the war against prejudice, but my focus in this book is on gender equality instead of racial equality.

What's Missing: A Linear History

Another noticeable absence is this book is a linear history of all women preachers in the IPHC or even in Oklahoma. At this time, others are working to gather and construct a history of women preachers in the IPHC that is not limited to just women in Oklahoma. My work is not as an historian, but as a rhetorical scholar who has one driving question: What role does ethos play in the autobiographical constructions of self for the IPHC women preachers? The value of this question is that the answers teach us something about ourselves, about God, and about the rich spiritual heritage of a community. While Pentecostalism is a lived, idiosyncratic experience, it is also part of a collective ethos as well. Thus, while it is fluid, its boundaries are also somewhat fixed. So, one Pentecostal cannot align himself completely outside of these rough boundaries and be a representative of the 'whole', nor can an individual within those boundaries carry so much weight that his or her experience determines the nature of Pentecostalism for all. Yet a close look at the unique autobiographies I reference reveals key

---

[6] Parham was a racist who rejected the Azusa Street revival. He was, however, the promulgator of tongues as the initial evidence for Spirit baptism (Harold D. Hunter, personal correspondence, May 26, 2010).

[7] In a recent conversation at the South Carolina IPHC Centennial Celebration, Bishop Ronald Carpenter stated that several African-American churches had become a part of the IPHC in Virginia. He said a current goal was to bring churches back to the IPHC that had split and become independent in the early 20th century.

strands of faith that tie us all together. These stories are fresh, new, and worthy of inclusion in our denomination's history. These stories teach us something important about the spiritual legacy left to us: it is always being reinvented and renewed in fresh visions carried out within the ministries of the IPHC.

What's Missing: A Discussion of the Effects of Religion in the Composition Classroom

Those in the field of Rhetoric and Composition, as this study is situated within English studies as opposed to Communication studies, will notice that I also do not address the topic of religion in the composition classroom, although my topic could easily encompass such a discussion. The attitudes we have about the role of religion in the composition classroom are indirectly addressed in this book because a discussion of composition pedagogy ultimately centers on a discussion of truth and the nature of epistemic rhetorics.[8] As a subset of theories of epistemic rhetoric, the theoretical framework I employ to reveal aspects of ethos engages with ideas about truth and the nature of knowledge production.

Even so, a brief look at the role of religion in the composition classroom is warranted because it has become a hotly debated topic as interest in the relationships between rhetoric and religions have increased. In 2007 Elizabeth Vander Lei and Lauren Fitzgerald published an article in the *Writing Program Administrator (WPA)* journal about the protection of the state from the church, that is, the silencing of religious discourse in the academy called 'What in God's Name?: Administering the Conflicts of Religious Belief in Writing Programs'.[9] Interpreted as a reoccurring problem by many compo-

---

[8] For discussions of how composition pedagogies are fed by an instructor's philosophical perspective on how knowledge is built, validated, and shared, and by extension on how truth is conceived in regard to these epistemological constructions, scholars can begin with James C. McDonald (ed.), *The Allyn and Bacon Sourcebook for College Writing Teachers* (New York: Longman, 2nd edn, 1999). The major sources of our knowledge of the nature and influence of epistemic rhetorics and the reaches and limitations of social constructionism as they relate to pedagogy in the composition classroom are named in the essays and their attendant bibliographies. These discussions began over twenty years ago and encapsulate what is common knowledge in my field at this time.

[9] Some readers will immediately notice the reversal of an old theme, that is, of protecting the church from the state, not the state from the church. Leading

sition teachers at all levels—from T.A.s to full professors—religion's intrusion into the composition classroom has been largely seen as a threat, as evidence of a student's irrational (i.e. colloquial/uneducated) belief system and as a way of perpetuating just the type of prejudices that liberal rhetoric and composition scholars hope to undermine.[10] While Vander Lei and Fitzgerald argue for inclusion, the impetus to write such an article points to an anti-Christian undercurrent in the field. In practice, the composition classroom is sometimes used as a place to silence religion while privileging social and political perspectives that run counter to the beliefs of many Christians in many denominations.

In fact, it is part of a trend designed effectively to demonize Christians by reducing all of them to one easily identifiable target before arguing for a secularized epistemological perspective. This perspective is then translated into praxis in the composition classroom, and a push for a liberal political and social agenda is made. For example, in David Wallace's 2009 article, 'Alternative Rhetoric and Morality: Writing From the Margins', the explicit call for composition teachers to begin undermining what is seen as *normative, white, privileged,* Christian discourse *that excludes homosexuals* and non-whites and thereby disempowers the members of these groups relies upon Wallace's use of this narrow definition of Christianity.[11] To claim Christianity is *normative* depends upon one's context. For Wallace, the world outside of the university seems to be dominated by Christians, but it is a common lament in churches today that many Americans are losing touch with their faith. So what is normative? Perhaps moral and social mediocrity is the norm, as ambiguous as that may sound.

---

intellectual Stephen Carter has written a number of influential books and articles on this topic. Visit this link to see a list of texts and to read a short biography: http://www.randomhouse.com/knopf/authors/carter/bio.html. A graduate of Yale with a degree in law, Carter has written *God's Name in Vain: The Wrongs and Rights of Religion in Politics* (New York: Basic Books, 2000) and *The Culture of Disbelief: How American Law and Politics Trivialize Religion* (New York: Basic Books, 1993).

[10] Elizabeth Vander Lei and Lauren Fitzgerald, 'What in God's Name? Administering the Conflicts of Religious Beliefs in Writing Programs', *WPA Writing Program Administration: Journal of the Council of Writing Program Administrators* 31.1-2 (Fall-Winter 2007), pp. 185-95.

[11] David L. Wallace, 'Alternative Rhetoric and Morality: Writing from the Margins', *College Composition and Communication* 61.2 (2009), pp. W18-39. The

In addition, it is reductive to assign a single *race* to Christianity. Many historians and theologians would quickly complicate such a reductive view of religion and power and, as we can already see from my brief introduction, race. Even within those Pentecostal denominations in the United States that are dominated by Caucasians, an explicit argument for racial equality is still being made. In my own town of Farmville, Virginia, the only church where both races comfortably come together to worship is the Pentecostal church New Life Assembly of God. While I did not think much of this at first, after spending the last three years here, I have come to understand that it is highly significant for African-Americans and Caucasians to worship together in a town that chose to close its public schools for five years in the 50s rather than to integrate them.[12]

Wallace's definition of Christians as *privileged* is called into question since it is common knowledge that many late nineteenth and early twentieth century Pentecostals were of the lower classes. It is true that many Pentecostals are comfortably middle-class today, but the legacy of humility is not forgotten in our histories or in our practice. However, Wallace does not necessarily confine his accusation of elitism to Christians, even accusing himself of it toward the end of his article. He does paint the world outside of the university as *homophobic*, implying that it is so because of white Christians. Yet, accusations of homophobia certainly don't hold either, as one can easily see by looking at a typical congregation in a Pentecostal church or in other Protestant churches who allow homosexuals to occupy a place in the congregation, although never within the church leadership. But homophobia is not the issue and it really hasn't been in a very long time; biblical exegesis is the issue and remains the issue as a brief look at articles published in *Christianity Today* will quickly reveal.

---

theme runs throughout the article, but specific mention of the white male is on page W22, and page W31 is a more specific discussion of his view.

[12] 'We may observe with much sadness and irony that, outside of Africa, south of the Sahara, where education is still a difficult challenge, the only places on earth known not to provide free public education are Communist China, North Viet Nam, Sarawak, Singapore, British Honduras—and Prince Edward County, Virginia. Something must be done about Prince Edward County' (Robert F. Kennedy, March 1963, cited at <http://www.mercyseatfilms.com/aboutfilm. html>).

What is significant about Wallace's article is that at this time, due to a lack of knowledge in areas such as history and theology (to varying degrees), other scholars in my field might also be tempted to reduce these histories and theologies into convenient labels and attach them to the umbrella term 'Christian' in order to mold an identifiable, weakened target. It is time Christian scholars begin to point out the ways Christians have been essentialized (to use a feminist term) because it is all too easy to find examples of how liberal scholars are increasingly using reductive labels to silence Christian points of view in academic journals, on secular campuses, and in classrooms.

To return to a discussion of how a brief look at how the rejection of Christianity in the composition classroom tangentially relates the overarching exploration of epistemic rhetorics that form the theoretical backbone of this book, it is worth also briefly looking at Wallace's reasons for making such a concerted, purposeful attempt to attack Christians. His views are not isolated, but they are representative of a growing mindset accepted by the most influential scholars within the field of rhetoric and composition.

The purpose for essentializing Christians becomes clear when Wallace says on the one hand we 'cannot substitute leftist political leanings' when searching for ways rhetoric has become 'complicit' in oppression, but on the other hand we need to construct 'alternative rhetorics that take as their central task the identification and unseating of inequities and that substantively account for the ways in which exercising rhetorical agency involves the responsibility of accounting for the impact of that agency on others'.[13] Even though he paradoxically tries to disassociate his liberal values from a political system and then use that de-politicized position to claim that the composition classroom can be a place for illustrating how the actions of those holding hegemonic positions must pay attention to those who are silenced or marginalized, the fact is that the composition classroom can never really be dislodged from its political contexts—not to mention religious and social contexts. Thus, Wallace's readers circle back to the start of the article. The goal is to unseat those identified as Christian, specifically white Christians who are assumed to be racist, elitist, and homophobic. And how will this be

---

[13] Wallace, *Alternative Rhetoric and Morality*, p. W35.

accomplished? From behind the safety of the politicized, secularized lectern of the composition classroom.[14]

Those outside of my field might find this debate confusing. After all, isn't the writing classroom supposed to be about … writing? Don't we talk about thesis statements, varieties of structure, the potential of academic and creative language, the medium of writing as a tool of learning as well as communication? Well, yes and no. Explicit acknowledgement of the use of the classroom as a place of political, social, and ultimately, religious transformation began back in the late 40s, as Ronald Clark Brooks describes in his 2009 article about two scholars who challenged the use of the composition classroom as a political soapbox, namely Richard Weaver and Maxine Hairston.[15] Whereas the college classroom used to be focused on content, the Brooks article shows us just how pervasive the mentality has become that we are to convert students to our own philosophical, political, and, as a tacit undercurrent, religious or anti-religious beliefs as we convey that content.[16]

---

[14] It is worth noting briefly that another example of an exploration of rhetoric and religion is Sharon Crowley's often-cited book, *Toward a Civil Discourse: Rhetoric and Fundamentalism* (Pittsburgh Series in Composition, Literacy, and Culture; Pittsburgh, PA: University of Pittsburgh Press, 2006). However, while praised by many in our field, she makes an error similar to the one made by David Wallace. By reducing a representation of Christianity to those who occupy a fundamentalist position and by specifically targeting those who believe in the second coming of Christ, Crowley manages to make Christians into an enemy who 'threatens the civil discourse necessary to democracy', as Brenda Glascott notes in a review of the book (*Composition Studies* 34.2 [Fall 2006], pp. 130-32). Again, Christianity is reduced to a simple definition, Christians are identified as ignorant (with apocalyptic belief as a symbol of just how irrational they are), and then Christians are made into a group who need to dialogue with liberals—not to Christianize liberals but to receive an 'education' from liberals by learning to understand and use reason. On the other hand, liberals, Crowley tells us, need to be educated by Christians and learn to accept 'emotion', 'affect', and 'opinion' as legitimate elements of the knowledge-making processes of rhetoric.

[15] Ronald Clark Brooks, 'Historicizing Critiques of Procedural Knowledge: Richard Weaver, Maxine Hairston, and Post-Process Theory', *College Composition and Communication* 61.1 (2009), pp. W90-106 (W90).

[16] In Lester Faigley's *Fragments of Rationality: Postmodernity and the Subject of Composition* (Pittsburgh, PA: University of Pittsburgh Press, 1992), he claims Richard Ohmann's 1976 *English in America* was a 'political analysis of English studies that stands out from its time like one of the sandstone monoliths over Monument Valley' (p. 132). Ohmann is quoted as writing that composition textbooks 'divorce writing from society, need, and conflict' and 'break [writing] down into a series of routines' (p. 132). Thus, attention to the political aspects of composition did not begin as an attack on conservativism or Christianity, but this has increas-

Brooks criticizes Richard Weaver for wanting to bring content into the composition classroom and for resisting the use of the composition classroom to 'bring about a more equitable social order'. In Brooks' opinion, Weaver's error was his belief that the teacher's job is to promote a type of Platonic dialectic in order to discover truth. However, in a field dominated by relativists the pervasive belief is that there is no existing truth to be discovered; there are only relative truths to be constructed.[17] As Brooks explains, 'progressive educators', unlike Weaver, want to use experience to lead students into the 'truth about the nature of the world'. 'Political progressivism' thus seeks the change liberals so desire since the truths constructed will be done in conjunction with the liberal views of the composition teacher.

To drive his point home that the composition classroom is now the place of conversion to an alternative epistemology, Brooks brings up Maxine Hairston's opposition in the 1990s to show that those who wish to use the composition classroom to convey knowledge about writing are not respected in our field. Instead, he advocates expressivist pedagogies, which lead to an expression of relative truths; and he leans toward political progressivism, which leads to the student's critical reflection on those values that don't align with what the instructor has chosen to emphasize during the course. Hairston's perspicacious accusation is quoted ('It's a model … that puts dogma before diversity, politics before craft, ideology before critical thinking, and the social goals of the teacher before the educational needs of the student') and then dismantled by Brooks in the remainder of the article.[18]

---

ingly become a theme today. The reaction was against teaching writing outside of its contexts and its ability to influence others when Ohmann published this text.

[17] Brooks, 'Historicizing Critiques of Procedural Knowledge', p. W95.

[18] Brooks, 'Historicizing Critiques of Procedural Knowledge', p. W99. David Horowitz notes the following: 'All higher education institutions in this country embrace principles of academic freedom that were first laid down in 1915 in the famous General Report of the American Association of University Professors, titled "The Principles of Tenure and Academic Freedom". The Report admonishes faculty to avoid "taking unfair advantage of the student's immaturity by indoctrinating him with the teacher's own opinions before the student has had an opportunity to fairly examine other opinions upon the matters in question, and before he has sufficient knowledge and ripeness of judgment to be entitled to form any definitive opinion of his own"' ('Why an Academic Bill of Rights is Necessary' [15 March 2005], <http://www.studentsforacademicfreedom.org/news/997/DHohiotestimony031505.html>).

My uncomfortable role as a Christian scholar, in light of the reductive definitions of Christianity at play, as well as the ugly accusations of racism, elitism, and homophobia associated with Christian
beliefs, should be more evident by now. Additionally, the presentation of a Christian epistemology through an exploration of the
ethos-making of IPHC women preachers might be interpreted by
secular scholars as a threat to those in the field who wish to disman-
tle, ridicule, and address any epistemological process that does not
lead to the social and political conclusions they wish to justify in the
composition classroom, in journals, and on campuses. However,
avoiding the topic of religion is not the answer. After all, religion is
not absent from composition studies, nor from composition classrooms, and certainly not from the minds of students.

In the end, Hairston made a good point: A classroom should be
more than a political soapbox for liberal teachers, no matter how
justified they feel their cause might be; but it is also a weak point
because the classroom can never be apolitical. Yet if politics must
be the undercurrent of composition pedagogies since the ways writing gets taught emerge from one's perception of truth and reality,
then let all voices be heard. We are to educate students by offering
them real choices in a critical reflection on their own ideological
perspectives instead of tipping the scales toward the political views
we most value. When the goal becomes conversion to the political
or religious views of a teacher (assuming one is teaching on a secular campus), a line is crossed.

What's Missing: Feminism

This brings me to another missing piece of this book. Most of the
scholars who learned of my research several years ago expected me
to take an explicitly feminist view. Like history, religion, and theology, feminism requires a great deal of study to understand it as a
historical, intellectual, and religious current that has adapted to its
changing environment over the years. Beyond that, religion is often-
the enemy in contemporary feminist studies, despite feminism's
conservative origins. To be clear, I do hold views that may comfortably be labeled as feminist, but I often refrain from using the
label since the term is so often associated with very vocal leftist
views.

Instead, in this book I focus on the use of Corder's theory of generative ethos to gain insights into how the IPHC women preachers constructed themselves in their autobiographies. While rhetoric, by its very nature, is a field fascinated by the study of power, in this book power is addressed with an open look at how the IPHC Christians worked together as well as to how gender issues were a challenge for them.[19] With that qualification, I do understand that any discussion of gender is rooted in centuries of arguments leading up to and supporting the equality of women. Again, the roots of feminism are distinctly Christian. Without the support of Christian women in the eighteenth and nineteenth centuries, the right to vote would never have been achieved; and the rights to property, education, protection from abuse, and one's earned wages might never have been successfully defended without the right to vote. Yet an explicit placement of the IPHC women within feminist histories and an engagement with or confrontation of feminist theories does not take center stage. Feminism is the backdrop, Christianity is the stage, and Corder's rhetorical theory of ethos provides the costumes for the actresses.

What's Missing: Kennedy and Burke

Although it seems that my field is just waking up to an exploration of the relationships between rhetoric and religion, scholars will also note that I have ignored two influential texts in particular: George Kennedy's *New Testament Interpretation Through Rhetorical Criticism*, published in 1984, and Kenneth Burke's *The Rhetoric of Religion: Studies in Logology*, published in 1961 and again in 1970. The omission of George Kennedy is significant since his book, *Classical Rhetoric and Its Christian and Secular Tradition: From Ancient to Modern Times*, is regularly used in courses on rhetoric. The omission of Kenneth Burke is

---

[19] For a discussion of the shift of feminism from the political right to the left, see Nancy F. Cott, *The Grounding of Modern Feminism* (New Haven, CT: Yale University Press, 1987). Also, Christina Hoff Summers has written several books that challenge the histories of feminism and the statistics used to hold up some claims made by feminists. Also see my article that argues Christians should not use the term to destroy the careers of ambitious women in the church: 'Post-1960s Pentecostalism and the Promise of a Future for Pentecostal Holiness Women Preachers', *Cyberjournal for Pentecostal-Charismatic Research* 16 (January 2007), <http://www.pctii.org/cyberj/cyberj16/welch.html>.

significant due to his pervasive influence on the field through several books he has written. A journal is dedicated to him, and more than one scholar has found an exploration of his work worthy of study through her dissertation.

The reason Kennedy is not used as a source in this book is that his work is representative of a type of rhetorical criticism that tries to guess at the author or editor's intent, 'the results' of that rhetoric, and how the Bible would have been read by those living in that time.[20] Many scholars would question one's ability to determine completely what an author intended, and the reconstruction of an ancient epistemology is difficult at best, as Kennedy freely admits.[21] The book is valuable because it makes the education of the Bible's editors and writers apparent by showing how they were trained in rhetoric as it was taught at the time.[22] It is not useful because it reiterates a misunderstanding of religion.

This misunderstanding is revealed when Kennedy writes that 'at the heart of it [the New Testament] lies authoritative proclamation, not rational persuasion', as is the case in similar religions.[23] 'Those who accept religious teachings generally do so because of their perception of certain qualities in the person who utters them and because of their intuitive response to the message', he writes. The error is that the focus on the human ignores the work of the Holy Spirit, but Kennedy claims: 'Rational speech, such as the civic rhetoric of Greek cities, is in contrast demonstrative, based on formally valid inference from accepted premises'.[24] To dismiss the presence of logic from the Christian religion is absurd. Certainly Lee Strobel's *The Case for Christ* reveals just how much logic underlies the New Testament's arguments.[25]

There is a spiritual dynamic of persuasion that is not simply 'intuition', as Kennedy labels it. The Holy Spirit is often represented metaphorically by fire, and the 'anointing' of a preacher is revealed when the Spirit animates the persuasive abilities of a messenger beyond what she can achieve on her own. Conversion is a rational as

---

[20] George Kennedy, *New Testament Interpretation Through Rhetorical Criticism* (Chapel Hill, NC: The University of North Carolina Press, 1984), p. 4.
[21] Kennedy, *New Testament Interpretation*, p. 5.
[22] See Kennedy, *New Testament Interpretation*, chapter five.
[23] Kennedy, *New Testament Interpretation*, p. 6.
[24] Kennedy, *New Testament Interpretation*, p. 6.
[25] Psalm 104.4; Heb. 1.7.

well as an irrational response to the Spirit speaking through a preacher. Burke's error is similar. He argues that the metaphysical nature of language produces belief and that when we are converted to a religion, we do so through this aspect of language, not out of response to an actual spiritual world.[26] Both Kennedy and Burke try to suggest how the Spirit works by explaining the Spirit in terms of the material world.

In conclusion, my field is just re-engaging with conversations that scholars in other fields have been engaging with for decades, and the scholars in my field often privilege philosophical views that are openly and harshly critical of Christian epistemologies. However, the type of rhetorical analysis I have done in this book has something to offer all of my readers. The insights into the changing beliefs of IPHC Pentecostals within this small representative group of individuals have much to offer in a discussion about rhetoric, religion, and gender. For scholars of rhetoric, a look at how the rhetorical tradition emerged within the contexts of a small group of Oklahomans (who represent the larger collective ethos of Pentecostals in the denomination as well as other Pentecostals from a variety of denominations) tells us something about how rhetoric on a small scale determines the direction of rhetoric on a large scale.

It is my hope that Christians outside of academia will find the interviews to be moving. It is also hoped that they will be enlightened by my conclusions about the emerging ethos of the IPHC and by the definition of Pentecostalism in the twenty-first century as shared by the IPHC's former Presiding Bishop James Leggett. Additionally, the documents I share are stories seldom told and views rarely heard. They should be of interest to scholars and the general public alike. Historians have opened their ears to ordinary voices of an historical period as they continue to map histories grounded in the experiences of the common person. This helps us understand the significance of the extraordinary leaders who tend to dominate the pages of our history books at this time. Finally, the presence of Christ in my life and in the lives of the Christians I studied is evident in this book. As a practicing Pentecostal Christian, it is my hope that my work will inspire other Christian students in the field

---

[26] Kenneth Burke, *The Rhetoric of Religion: Studies in Logology* (Berkeley: University of California Press, 1970), pp. 16-17, 37.

of rhetoric and composition, and it is my hope that all readers will hear Christ's voice in these pages.

1

RHETORIC, GENDER, AND RELIGION

To fear the Lord is to hate evil. Pride, arrogance, evil ways, subversive talk, all those I hate. From me [the voice of wisdom] come advice and ability; understanding and power are mine (Prov. 8.13-14).

The Adventure Begins

Shortly after my son's birth in 2003, I enrolled at the University of Arizona in an eighteenth-nineteenth century history of rhetoric class taught by Thomas Miller, a well-known scholar of rhetoric.[1] As we read works by Margaret Fell and Phoebe Palmer, I became interested in women preachers. When I talked with my mother about my new interest in women preachers, she pointed out that the International Pentecostal Holiness Church had always accepted women as preachers. She also suggested that there might even be some materials in my grandfather's library that could help me. So, I made the thousand mile journey from Tucson to Oklahoma City that semester to peruse a library I had never found intriguing in the thirty years I'd spent living within a mile of it.

While at home, I met with Harold Hunter, Pentecostal Specialist and Director of the Archives at the International Pentecostal Holiness Church (IPHC) Resource Development Center in Oklahoma City, Oklahoma.[2] He directed me to various materials in the archives and later e-mailed me a bibliography of over a hundred books and

---

[1] Miller is currently the Associate Provost for Faculty Affairs at the University of Arizona. He won the 1998 Mina Shaugnessy award for his book, *The Formation of College English: Rhetoric and Belles Lettres in the British Cultural Provinces* (Pittsburgh Series in Composition, Literacy, and Culture; Pittsburgh, PA: University of Pittsburgh Press, 1997).

[2] Hunter's *Curriculum Vitae* is available at <http://www.pctii.org/vita.html>.

articles to help me get started seriously researching the subject. I knew nothing of the church's history. I felt that I had lived it through my grandmother's stories, my grandfather's life as a Pentecostal preacher, and my own experiences growing up Pentecostal; but from talking to Hunter I found out that I had much to learn. That semester changed my life. Between the richness of Tom Miller's course and the generous guidance of Harold Hunter, I began research that would become the subject of my dissertation, of many conference presentations, of several published articles, and of course, of the culmination of my work to date in this book.

At this time in the summer of 2010, I feel that I have come to the end of the first part of my journey. In the summer of 2009 I felt that, with a nearly final draft of this book, I had reached the final stages of this initial exploration into women preachers. The feeling was solidified by the July 2009 IPHC General Conference because it marked the end of my mother's thirty-year long employment with the IPHC, during which time she worked for three bishops, including the one presiding at that conference. At that same conference, I gave a speech to eighty-five people attending the Archives Banquet.[3] In January of 2011, I will again speak on women preachers at the IPHC Centennial Celebration in Falcon, North Carolina. When I speak, I hope to be holding a printed copy of this book in my hand.

The First of the Three Threads: Rhetoric

The idea that the autobiographies and transcribed interviews of IPHC women preachers who did not hold high positions in the

---

[3] A short summary of my presentation was included in the *IPHC Experience*. Readers can access the article at <http://www.iphcexperience.com/_pdfs/2009/Experience_Oct09.pdf>. An article I wrote for the *IPHC Experience*, called 'Our Spiritual Heritage: IPHC Women Called to Preach', is forthcoming. It includes some parts of the speech made at the Archives Banquet. One final note on the banquet presentation that I would like to make is that Harold Hunter's wife and secretary decorated the room beautifully. Crosses and candles sat on every table, with the candles giving off a beautiful light. But what was especially wonderful is that every single table included a framed photograph of an IPHC woman preacher. I had no idea such care would go into setting the stage for my presentation, but Sondra Hunter shared a story with me after the presentation about how Dr. Hunter had defended the right of women to preach from the earliest days of his career. The subject is a special one for the Hunters.

church nor take up many lines in IPHC history books do not con-
stitute a significant area of study is an idea that is not supported by
current scholarship in my field. In Tom Miller's seminal essay, 'Reinventing Rhetorical Traditions', he writes that the claim that there
is a singular rhetorical tradition to be studied is a 'fiction that has
just about outlasted its usefulness'. Instead, he suggests that we
should study the 'rhetoric of traditions'—that is, how different
communities 'maintain the shared values and assumptions that
authorize discourse' within those communities.[4] To continue treat-
ing the writers of the canonized works as if they were all writing
and thinking about rhetoric in the same way, under the same political, social, and historical conditions, is an over-simplification of
rhetoric which we instead understand to be a social praxis.[5] In fact,
an exploration of the changing contexts of the IPHC writers is
relevant for understanding how they structure their ethos, and a description of how the writers operate within those contexts will provide a way for understanding how these communities create knowledge and verify truth. Most importantly, the analysis of local communities allows scholars to view the more global accounts of rhetorical practices differently and offers some insight into how
women construct themselves in positions of power.

Visiting the IPHC archives and conducting my own interviews
has allowed me to offer new information to the field at large because the local communities operate in relationship to larger communities. Miller suggests that rhetorical scholars abandon the practice of literary critics which engage us in creating new readings of
old texts and instead engage with the work of historians who do
much more work gathering and analyzing new source materials in
localized communities. A rhetorical analysis of the rhetorics of local communities tells us more about the globalized practices of
rhetors speaking within and for the community at large.[6] Thus, the
rhetorics of Oklahoma women preachers can tell us something
about the rhetorics of women preachers separated by time and distance. These disparate voices form a community of women and

---

[4] Thomas P. Miller, 'Reinventing Rhetorical Traditions', in Theresa Enos (ed.),
Learning From the Histories of Rhetoric: Essays in Honor of Winifred B. Horner,
(Carbondale, IL: Southern Illinois University Press, 1993), pp. 26-41.

[5] Miller, 'Reinventing Rhetorical Traditions', pp. 27-28.

[6] Miller, 'Reinventing Rhetorical Traditions', pp. 28-29.

men speaking for equality in global contexts, but really to understand the ethos of the global community, one must analyze the rhetorics of a local community.

The need for new histories can be stated in terms of the effects of new histories. From these new histories that are built upon the voices of the ordinary participants, we can see that localized and globalized dialectics among Christian leaders create Christian epistemologies that battle for ideological hegemony, silencing or marginalizing dissenters. Analysis of such how communities create knowledge and verify truth are key to understanding how women, the intellectual and spiritual equals of men, have been put into marginalized positions by rhetorical practices that justify these prejudices.

Using rhetorical analysis as a research method involves rich descriptions of the social contexts of the writers. In support of Tom Miller's views on defining rhetorical traditions, Richard Graff and Michael Leff conclude:

> Communities develop forms of rhetorical practice that can be appreciated only when accompanied by thick description of the social contexts in which they arose and to which they responded. Suitably contextualized, the diverse forms of socially situated rhetorical practice can be characterized as traditions in their own right.[7]

Contexts such as audience descriptions, the political and historical situations of the writers, and emerging religious doctrines and practices were essential for characterizing the small group of IPHC writers from Oklahoma whom I chose to study.

While context is a central concern of rhetorical analysis, so are the theories that define how persuasion occurs. The term 'ethos' is often defined reductively in common usage, in textbooks for teaching freshman composition, and in the work of some scholars outside of the field of rhetoric or other fields that explore the far-reaching historical and culturally-embedded definitions and uses of 'ethos'. The reductive, simplified definition of ethos is essentially that ethos is a persuasive tool that is used in a speech or a text to

---

[7] Richard Graff and Michael Leff, 'Revisionist Historiography and Rhetorical Tradition(s)', in Richard Graff, Arthur Walzer, and Janet Atwill (eds.), *The Viability of the Rhetorical Tradition* (Albany, NY: SUNY Press, 2005), pp. 11-30 (23).

convince an audience of the speaker's goodwill, expertise, and authority. Using that definition, freshman composition students are instructed to look for any reference to a speaker's education, years of experience, evidence of expertise, and other indicators to see ethos in a text. However, the term is much more complex than that. In *The Art of Rhetoric*, when Aristotle describes ethos as a means of argument, he does so with the assumption that ethos is to be adjusted according to the reality of the audience at the time of the actual speech. Ethos is not a static tool but a dynamic construction that bridges the orator's art, her attempts at preparation, and the unpredictable reality of an audience grounded in a particular time and place.

James May describes three types of Aristotelian ethos: (1) that which exhibits intelligence, goodwill, arête, and virtue; (2) the character of the audience; and (3) the creation of the speaker's character in the speech and/or the creation of the defendant's character in his speech.[8] In Aristotle's view of rhetoric, one of the earliest attempts to describe the nature and practice of rhetoric, we see that ethos is dependent upon both audience and speaker; and it changes according to its context. Thus, rhetoric is ever changing, and both rhetor and auditor play roles in the shaping of a text or speech.

In the twentieth century, Jim Corder's theories of ethos were grounded in the stream of ever-emerging understandings of rhetoric and the role of ethos within those theories. Since Aristotle, ethos went through definitions that defined it as a permanent, inherited characteristic (Roman), as a construction (Renaissance), as a psychological tool (eighteenth-nineteenth centuries), and as a part of symbol-making and usage (twentieth century). Thus, when Corder writes about ethos, the term is fully enmeshed in an understanding of rhetoric as a tool of knowledge-making and in an understanding of language as a symbolic system (semiotics). Rhetoric's Burkean iterations characterize it as a bridge-building art, which attempts to overcome aspects of division by finding places of identification, and as a public act on a stage—planned, performed, and respon-

---

[8] James M. May, 'Ethos and Ciceronian Oratory', *Trials of Character: The Eloquence of Ciceronian Ethos* (Chapel Hill: University of North Carolina Press, 1998), pp. 1-12.

sive.[9] Thus in 'Varieties of Ethical Argument', Jim Corder defines several types of ethos because of the many ways of looking and thinking about rhetoric he had at his fingertips. The type of ethos I used as an analytical lens in this book is called 'generative ethos'.

The characteristics of generative ethos are as follows:

- *It can sometimes incorporate both a sense of the past and a sense of the future in a text.* An understanding of the dynamic of generative ethos includes a sense of how 'present actions thrust themselves into the future'.[10]

- *It resists espousing a singular viewpoint.* Generative ethos can sometimes resist espousing a 'bound' or singular viewpoint that leaves the discourse without a final resolution or answer(s). It moves 'toward completeness but beyond closure'.

- *It can act as an element of transformation* as the reader's qualities emerge while progressing through a text and also while working her way through the argument reflectively.

- *It can act as a tool of identification* yet retain the author's convictions.

- *It assumes that the message is always integrally related to the speaker or writer.* Corder writes that he does not support the idea that a writer/speaker can send a clear, singular message to a recipient, though she can limit meanings by the words chosen; but neither does he support the idea that once a message is spoken or written it leaves the speaker or writer. He quotes Walter Ong's statement that 'all words projected from a speaker remain, as has been seen, somehow interior to him, being an invitation to another person, another interior, to share the speaker's interior, an invitation to enter in, not to regard from the outside'.[11] 'Our words never leave us', writes Corder; 'the message is not separate from the speaker'.

---

[9] Kenneth Burke's works include *A Grammar of Motives* (New York: Prentice-Hall, 1945), *A Rhetoric of Motives* (New York: Prentice-Hall, 1950), and *The Rhetoric of Religion: Studies in Logology* (Berkeley, CA: University of California Press, 1970), among many others.

[10] Jim Corder, 'Varieties of Ethical Argument, With Some Account of the Significance of Ethos in the Teaching of Composition', in Richard E. Young and Yameng Liu (eds.), *Landmark Essays on Rhetorical Invention in Writing* (Davis, CA: Hermagoras Press, 1994), pp. 99-134 (114-126).

[11] Cited by Corder, 'Varieties of Ethical Argument', p. 127.

- *Generative ethos creates the speaker and creates her world; it invites the hearer into that world.* Speaking is not simply about communicating a message but about creating identification, understanding, and a shared world.
- *It is commodious* when other types of ethos, such as gratifying ethos, are not. It is commodious, whereas practices such as speaking in unknown tongues that cannot be interpreted by hearers are not.
- Finally, because it creates a world for the hearer to join, *it must be said that truth is made out of what is incomplete or partial.*

I made use of these characteristics to define some interpretive categories for analyzing the role of ethos in the texts and transcribed interviews of the IPHC women preachers. Forming a framework of categories allowed me to focus on particular aspects of the autobiographical texts and to investigate the texts themselves. Although my interpretation is subjective and my conclusions 'depend upon the frameworks from which they are perceived', establishing interpretive categories as a framework allowed me to build a 'descriptive relational hermeneutic' as a way of building knowledge about a subject.[12] Therefore, as a descriptive relational hermeneutic, the five elements of ethos that I used include:

1. ethos as a statement of motive or purpose(s) for composing the text/giving the interview;
2. ethos as a tool of transformation or ethos as an attempt to transform the reader;
3. ethos as the voice of wisdom or authority;
4. ethos as evidence of charisma; and
5. ethos as a bridge to identification with the reader through a dynamic process.

The Second of the Three Threads: Religion

Corderian ethos is set within the field of larger theories about the nature of rhetoric and truth, that is, within our current debates on

---

[12] Gary Backhaus and John Murungi, *Earth Ways: Framing Geographical Meanings* (Lanham, MD: Lexington Books, 2004), pp. xiv, xvii-xviii. I used Backhaus' explanation of how he structured his qualitative research as an early guide in how to structure my own research.

the nature of epistemic rhetorics. A brief sketch of how Corder's theory might be situated on this broad field is worth briefly addressing. Naturally, one of the biggest pieces to the puzzle of how and why women have been accepted as preachers in the IPHC is inherently tied to how truths are created and validated within the IPHC. Part of Corderian generative ethos assumes that creating and validating truth is a process constantly in flux, though perhaps with some guiding sense of right and wrong. Understanding fully that the nature of truth is a complex and contested area of study, I will proceed in this book with the assertion that truth can be relative but it can be absolute as well, and often it is context that determines the difference. Epistemic rhetorics, that is, those arguments deployed to build or to tear down knowledge, are examples of how generative ethos works in the art of persuasion with the goal of generating, validating, or challenging relative or absolute truths.

Four major rhetorical perspectives are described by James Berlin in his landmark essay, 'Contemporary Composition: The Major Pedagogical Theories'. These rhetorical perspectives will illustrate briefly how the understanding of rhetoric and its relationship to truth have emerged and how that impacts our understanding of rhetoric in the ethos-making of IPHC women preachers. The four categories are tied up in Berlin's references to some major trends in composition theory as well. They are: (1) Aristotelian, (2) Current-Traditional, (3) Neo-Platonic, and (4) the New Rhetoric or Epistemic Rhetoric. In the article Berlin authored, a discussion of the relationship between one's view of reality, language, meaning, writer (as opposed to author), and audience are used to explain differences in these four perspectives and ultimately to argue for the last one, for Epistemic Rhetoric.[13] The article ultimately serves as a summary of the major dispositions of scholars in the field of rhetoric and composition and reveals how I am working both within and beyond the constraints of these dispositions to make a place for religion within the theories of epistemic rhetorics.

---

[13] James A. Berlin, 'Contemporary Composition: The Major Pedagogical Theories', *College English* 44 (December 1982), pp. 765-77 (reprinted in Victor Villanueva, Jr. [ed.], *Cross-Talk in Comp Theory: A Reader* [Urbana, IL: NCTE, 1997], pp. 1-19).

James Berlin writes, 'To teach writing is to argue for a version of reality, and the best way of knowing and communicating it'.[14] Although I don't focus on the role of ethos in the composition classroom in this book, it is easy to draw a parallel between Berlin's ideas about teaching composition and a preacher's calling to share her life in the pulpit and in the texts she leaves us. Ultimately, to preach from a pulpit is to argue for a version of reality and for the schemata that will be used to validate it, and to write an autobiography is to share a version of reality, not just details of a life.

In his discussion of four major perspectives on rhetoric that determine how we think of composition and, by extension, our world, Berlin succinctly places rhetoric in some broad philosophical contexts. In Aristotelian rhetoric, reality is understood to exist independently of the observer and can be discovered through sense impressions. Using reason, the rhetor can deductively arrive at truth, and truth can be clearly communicated through language.[15] A composition teacher operating out of this philosophical perspective teaches that writing is a relatively unproblematic tool of communication.

In Current-Traditional rhetoric, 18th century Scottish Common Sense realism is emphasized. This pedagogy is associated with the writing process formula, that is, the idea that good writing comes from simply following the prewriting, outlining, drafting, and revision process. In this epistemology, knowledge is generated through a 'simple correspondence between sense impressions and the faculties of the mind'. Unlike Aristotelian rhetoric, truth is discovered through inductive reasoning validated by 'observation and experiment'. Like Aristotelian rhetoric, truth is to be discovered outside of the rhetorical enterprise using the scientific method or one's own genius to find it.[16] So, the goal is to convey convincingly these discovered truths to the audience. Truth is known and verifiable, not probabilistic.[17]

In reaction to Scottish Common Sense Realism, Neo-Platonic expressionists assert that they can find truth themselves but can't communicate it except by analogy to their readers. They too believe

---

[14] Berlin, 'Contemporary Composition', p. 766.
[15] Berlin, 'Contemporary Composition', p. 767.
[16] Berlin, 'Contemporary Composition', pp. 769-70.
[17] Berlin, 'Contemporary Composition', p. 770.

in the existence of verifiable truths but find them in personal experience, not sense experience.[18] Much expressivist writing instruction encourages dialectical interaction between writers and readers in the search for truths. Expressivists throw away formulas or at least mix them up and seek to find the 'authentic voice' in a piece of writing, rather than to use the writing to find universal truths. Individual truths are privileged in this classroom.

None of these approaches to understanding reality or communicating it are wholly acceptable to Berlin. Today, he tells us, the New Rhetoric or Epistemic Rhetoric departs from these theories by viewing 'rhetoric as epistemic, that is, as a means of arriving at truth'. He writes:

> Truth is always truth for someone standing in relation to others in a linguistically circumscribed situation. The elements of the communication process [writer, reader, reality, language, meaning] do not simply provide a convenient way for talking about rhetoric. They form the elements that go into the very shaping of knowledge.

Truth is not discoverable because it always has to be organized through language in order to have meaning. He argues that language 'embodies and generates truth' and that 'truth is dynamic and dialectical', not just a thing to be retrieved from the outside world. Instead, it is 'created, not pre-existent and waiting to be discovered'.[19]

Berlin builds on scholarship dating back to the 60s when he defines his understanding of epistemic rhetoric. In 1967, Robert Scott 'rekindled the sophistic vision of rhetoric's relationship to truth, arguing that rhetoric is epistemic'.[20] Essentially, Scott argued that we should see 'argument as a process of generating time-limited truths'. Later, Barry Brummett would support him with the argument that 'even scientific observation is mediated by observational devices ... or recording devices' that 'always introduce limiting and biasing perspectives'; an argument that rips away science's attempt

---

[18] Berlin, 'Contemporary Composition', pp. 771-72.
[19] Berlin, 'Contemporary Composition', pp. 772-74.
[20] John Louis Lucaites, Celeste Michelle Condit, and Sally Caudill (eds.), *Contemporary Rhetorical Theory: A Reader* (London: The Guilford Press, 1999), p. 128.

to offer us facts in a world tested by and interpreted by imperfect people.[21] Brummet argues,

> The production of knowledge and reality is typically a collective or 'intersubjective' process, rather than a simple matter of each of us deciding for ourselves what is true. And it is precisely in this context that he argues that rhetoric provides the best model for producing and understanding the intersubjectivity of knowledge, truth, and reality.[22]

It is true that the social construction of knowledge makes sense and can easily be verified if we search the realms of our personal experience, without giving too much thought to possible exceptions. The problem is that, with the purging of universal truths, with the destruction of all facts, and with the rejection of any kind of a reality that exists outside of the mind, God is discarded too.

Even though scholars like Berlin can comfortably situate themselves in the definition of epistemic rhetoric that they offer, the definition is really not that simple. As Richard Cherwitz and James Hikins point out, 'not even the most committed subjectivist would support the thesis that reality is *purely* a mental construct by venturing into the path of an oncoming locomotive'.[23] As they go through perspectives on truth and reality in an article that effectively poked holes in much of Robert Scott's theory, the ultimate question emerges: Does language construct the world? Such a question might be quickly followed by: Or is it pre-existing and discovered? In the end, one has to ask: Does language simply construct an interpretation of a discovered world? Social constructivists, intersubjectivists, and rhetoricians like Berlin and Scott lean toward 'yes' in answer to the first question. Objectivists, scientists, Aristotelians, Platonists, and Christians lean toward 'yes' to the second question. A 'yes' to the third question is representative of a middle ground that might be occupied by many from these groups. The problem is that if a view allows room for the existence of God, then one might argue that not only is there a preexisting reality that could have been created by God but also there is a preexisting moral reality that chal-

---

[21] Lucaites, Condit, and Caudill, *Contemporary Rhetorical Theory*, pp. 128-29.

[22] Lucaites, Condit, and Caudill, *Contemporary Rhetorical Theory*, p. 129.

[23] Richard Cherwitz and James Hikins, 'Rhetorical Perspectivism', in Lucaites, Condit, and Caudill (eds.), *Contemporary Rhetorical Theory*, pp. 176-93 (177).

lenges the ideologies the social constructivist view supports. The battle over an agreed upon definition of epistemic rhetoric is an ideological battle as well as a philosophical one.

While Berlin's idea of epistemic rhetoric is useful and while Cherwitz and Hikin's ideas about epistemic rhetoric are fair, in my opinion, Pentecostals allow room for universal truths that come from a being outside of and not created by language. As in the Aristotelian view, reality can be discovered; it's not just created through social interaction and community consensus. Our 'a priori' deity spoke us into being, not the other way around. The creation of ethos in the autobiographies of women preachers is evidence of how reality is constructed by a community, but the conclusion that we are born as 'blank slates' who are not endowed with a nature, a soul, and a 'calling' on our lives given to us by God would be false. When the author of *Proverbs* writes that love of God is essentially the hatred of evil, the acknowledgement of a moral order is paramount. When he writes that wisdom grants 'advice and ability', 'understanding and power', it means that real wisdom cannot be generated by humans without the help of a spiritual entity such as God. To think of generative ethos in the lives of women preachers outside of this context would be wrong. Whatever Corder's spiritual views may or may not have been, for the Pentecostal Christian, life is *of* the spirit, *in* the spirit, *empowered* by the spirit, and *educated* by the spirit. It is the material world that is secondary, not the spiritual one.

Nevertheless, the growth of the community resulted in interactions that set ground rules for defining a Pentecostal reality—in particular, that the baptism of the Holy Spirit is real and life-changing—and the rules for how one could generate and validate doctrinal truths in relationship to the reality recognized and experienced by the group. In some ways, the validation of Pentecostal ethos meant adherence to the rules of the reality they had generated together and are still in the process of generating. In other ways, their ethos was evidence of the work of God, begun as soon as life began in the womb, as Psalm 139 reminds us. Additionally, divine revelation and other types of communication with God played a role in Pentecostal rhetorics. While most scholars in my field prefer to work with the material world alone, my rhetorical analysis must also account for the spiritual. In a way, this is the real work of a rhetorician if we look back to the work of Richard Weaver.

In 1963 Richard Weaver delivered a lecture at the University of Oklahoma called 'Language is Sermonic'.[24] In this lecture, delivered in the last year of his life, Weaver said:

> We need to recall that the great success of scientific or positivistic thinking in the Nineteenth century produced a belief that nothing was beyond the scope of its method. Science ... was doing so much to alter and, it was thought, to improve the material conditions of the world, that a next step with the same process seemed in order. Why should not science turn its apparatus upon man, whom all the revelations of religion and the speculations of philosophy seemed still to have left an enigma? ... It came to be believed increasingly that to think validly was to think scientifically, and that subject matters made little difference.[25]

However, we are not primarily or solely persuaded by logic, he argued. As the 'most humanistic of the humanities', rhetoric is about 'the whole man'. Rhetoric is human; it is historically, socially, religiously situated; it is about relationships. 'Rhetoric always comes to us in well-fleshed words, and that is because it must deal with the world, the thickness, stubbornness, and power of it'.[26] Deeply influenced by, although politically opposed to, atheist Kenneth Burke, he quotes him saying, 'All rhetoric is a rhetoric of motives', and objectivity is present only in degrees within any discourse.[27] But by the end of his rich discussion of rhetoric, he described language as 'sermonic' and rhetoricians as 'preachers in private or public capacities'.[28]

Rhetoricians are preachers because, in Weaver's view: 'We have no sooner uttered words than we have given impulse to other people to look at the world, or some small part of it, in our way'. Because we are all motivated by a scheme of values, 'we must never lose sight of the order of values as the ultimate sanction of rheto-

---

[24] Richard Weaver, 'Language is Sermonic', in Patricia Bizzell and Bruce Herzberg (eds.), *The Rhetorical Tradition: Readings From Classical Times to the Present* (Boston: Bedford/St. Martin's, 2d edn, 2001), p. 1349. I find it interesting that Weaver's speech was given in Oklahoma, the setting of my study, and that this speech was delivered in the last year of his life.

[25] Weaver, 'Language is Sermonic', p. 1352.

[26] Weaver, 'Language is Sermonic', p. 1353.

[27] Weaver, 'Language is Sermonic', p. 1359.

[28] Weaver, 'Language is Sermonic', p. 1360.

ric'. As practitioners, we operate as preachers because we guide others toward one end or another.[29] In short, Weaver argues that rhetoric is about ethics and that ethics don't respond to the cold perspective of science that would endeavor to reduce all things to formulaic actions and responses. Thus, we cannot ignore what can't be quantified and reduced to 'fact'. Scholars of rhetoric must engage with humanity in all of its complexity, and to discount the ethos of those of us who hold to religious faiths as 'lesser than' those scholars claiming to be materialists is to discount those of us who are operating out of what it really means to be fully human for humanity is both rational and irrational.

The Final Thread: Gender

Perhaps gender will be the most prominent of the three threads that have been intertwined to make this book. Since it is explicated in relationship to the texts I studied, I will not go into the details of how gender is defined here. Needless to say, I have confined myself to a traditional treatment of gender and a conservative, Christian understanding of how gender should be within our society. I understand the limits of such a perspective.

In conclusion, even though I am endeavoring to characterize the epistemic rhetoric of Oklahoma IPHC women preachers by an analysis of the dynamic of generative ethos within their autobiographical texts, I do not mean to be reductive in my characterization. In the summer of 2009 I spent a weekend at the Rhetoric Society of America's summer institute. Over three sessions I met with scholars who wanted to discuss what 'The Sacred in the 21st Century' might mean. One of the key themes that emerged was that we each had an idiosyncratic experience of our faith. We also came to an open realization that our knowledge was partial. Thus, my knowledge is fragmented in this text and my views of Pentecostalism are often idiosyncratic. Such a position is common. Historian Allan Anderson writes, 'Pentecostals have defined themselves by so many paradigms that diversity itself has become a primary defining

---

[29] Weaver, 'Language is Sermonic', p. 1360.

characteristic'.[30] It is only in classical Pentecostalism that simpler definitions can be somewhat effectively employed.[31]

It is not the purpose of this book to give a final, definitive answer on what it means to be Pentecostal or even on what it means to be a Christian. The apostle Paul writes, 'For our knowledge and our prophecy alike are partial, and the partial vanishes when wholeness comes' (1 Cor. 13.9, 10) and 'My knowledge now is partial; then it will be whole, like God's knowledge of me' (1 Cor. 13.12). My interpretation of Christian epistemology involves acknowledging that we are, and will remain, only partially aware of all there is to know. My idiosyncratic experience of faith means that I will never be able fully to render a picture of the whole for the women of the IPHC.

Telling the IPHC's story through these texts reveals so much more than just a rendition of events and the assertion that women should be included in the telling of the story. It reveals how these Pentecostals viewed life and how they became the spiritual ancestors of the next generation and then the next and the next. It is my hope that their legacy will be carried out in the histories of our denomination as well as be discussed in the field of rhetoric I hold so dear.

---

[30] Allan Anderson, *An Introduction to Pentecostalism* (Cambridge, UK: Cambridge University Press, 2007), p. 10.

[31] Anderson, *An Introduction to Pentecostalism*, p. 10.

2

WE ARE OF THIS PLACE: OKLAHOMA AND ETHOS

There I shall give you shepherds after my own heart, and they will lead you with knowledge and understanding (Jer. 3.15).

Making Connections

My own Pentecostalism is distinctly 'Oklahoman'. I've spent the last seven years of my life driving back to Oklahoma to become centered again by reconnecting with my family and the goodness of the place itself. I can always tell when I'm getting close to the state line because the wind starts pushing on the car, and I have to drive against it. As I speed down the highway fighting the wind, I love to see the rolling plains of wheat, the pastures with horses and cattle quietly grazing, the unimpeded horizon bending to the curve of the earth. As the beauty of my home state sinks into my bones, I often feel the words of my favorite Oklahoma poet whisper in my soul: 'I am a feather on the bright sky/ I am the blue horse that runs in the plain', and my soul is transformed by the blur of red clay telling me that I am of this place, that I am this place, that I have come home. Momaday's 'delight song' crescendos with the refrain:

> You see I am alive, I am alive/
> I stand in good relation to the earth/
> I stand in good relation to the gods/
> I stand in good relation to all that is beautiful.[1]

---

[1] N. Scott Momaday, 'The Delight Song of Tsoai-talee', *The Poetry Foundation*, <http://www.poetryfoundation.org/archive/poem.html?id=175895>. Momaday taught at the University of Arizona where I earned my PhD. However, I never

Through his language, the harmony of body, soul, God and earth is captured perfectly. Ironically, it is my long separation from home that has revealed the harmony to me.

I did not see my own experiences with God as a native Oklahoman as being unique until my move from Oklahoma took me out west—way out west and way down south to about an hour's drive north of the Mexican border. Situated in the northern region of the Sonoran desert, Tucson, Arizona, is full of life, even in the sweltering summer heat. Most mornings, I would see quail and the occasional wild jackrabbit scurrying through my yard. The quail and jackrabbits would quietly visit the water dish my husband filled for them; they would drink but be watchful and tense in the morning air. By midmorning, I loved to spy on a jackrabbit, sprawled out on his back, with his long feet relaxed onto the rocky, cool sand under our orange tree. In the quiet of the desert, we often had geckos in the house; they were uninvited guests who froze for a moment when spotted, in that classic stance with their tiny tails curved in a C. When it rained, an army of red ants would march across the middle of our driveway to pick up the bright, reddish pink petals dropped from the spiny, thin limbs of the Ocotillo whose arms reached over eight feet into the clear desert sky. I remember this tiny stream of ants, silently flowing in on one side and then out on the other with the red petals floating above their small bodies. Nothing we did could keep them from coming, so we finally gave up trying.

On rare but special occasions, I would see a gray coyote gazing steadily at me several feet away from among a riverbed of soft, round stones as I went out to gather my mail. I didn't fear him like I feared the javelinas who sometimes came out at dusk to forage from the orange tree. The silence and slow momentum of life was so different under the desert sun. There was no wind to wake us up and no seasons to mark. A saguaro, towering high in the sky, had stood guard in my front yard perhaps before our old house was even built. The barrel cactus and desert broom and the rock-filled

---

had time to take the class he occasionally taught. He was not an active member of the faculty but more of a peripheral figure. I don't recall ever seeing him on campus during the five years I was there.

yard all spoke to me of a new life and a new earth to understand and come to know.

Perhaps the clearest difference between my home in the desert and my home in Oklahoma can be seen by a contrast of spring-time weather. In Oklahoma, instead of calm springs brought in by mists of rain, spring would rip through with violent storms that left the landscape choked with long, lush blades of green grass and a dewy array of red, blue, lavender, and yellow wildflowers. In Oklahoma, the spring-time rain sometimes fell in impenetrable sheets and the wind came quickly alive, dangerously alive. What might be merely violent on one night could be deadly on another.

Some people feared these storms, especially when they produced tornadoes. Although I rarely fled to the basement when a tornado warning was issued on the news, I vividly remember smelling gas fumes carried on the wild, thick air in the aftermath of the famous tornadoes of 3 May 1999 that devastated parts of Moore. Standing silently on my porch that day in May, I was reminded of my own insignificance as I observed the solid, gray clouds easing their way across the sky while the remainder of its violent winds, lessened by the miles between my front porch and the target of its vigor, force-fully teased at my body. It is as much through destruction as through the abundance of life that I grew up knowing the power of God is something to be taken seriously.

Indeed, the Pentecostal Holiness religion, my religion, is like these Oklahoma storms. The storms are life and they are death. Through these storms it seems that all of the supernatural enti-ties—both good and evil—are real to me. Only after sitting beneath the calm, Arizona sun have I come to see how different the God of the desert is from the God of the Oklahoma storms, how the expe-rienced story of my life as a Christian in Tucson was different from my life as a Christian in Oklahoma. Therefore, it is not just from theory but from my perspective as an Oklahoman, as a Christian, and as a scholar of rhetoric, that I have come to believe that ethos is shaped both by a place and by its inhabitants. My understanding of what it means to be Pentecostal is distinctly and irrevocably 'Ok-lahoman'.

Putting an 'Oklahoman' Ethos into Perspective

Pentecostalism is certainly not confined to the borders of Oklahoma, nor is it the same homemade concoction of experience and religion on the frontier as it once was in the early twentieth century. Allan Anderson cites estimates that Pentecostals and Charismatics 'have become the largest numerical force in world Christianity after the Roman Catholic Church and represent a quarter of all Christians'. Less than a century after the Azusa Street revivals of 1906, there are more than 'five hundred million adherents worldwide', and perhaps there are even more today.[2] Historian Vinson Synan gives a bit more conservative estimate, explaining that although Pentecostalism began with only a 'handful of people in 1901',[3] it now has over two hundred million members and is 'exceeded in number by only the Roman Catholics'.[4] More than five hundred million people comprise those who are charismatic within Pentecostal, mainline, and Roman Catholic churches.[5]

Today, the sheer number of practicing Pentecostals and the global character of Pentecostalism tell us that the stereotype of Pentecostals should no longer be reduced to the portrayal of Pentecostals through examples like preacher Betty Lou Carter in Harvey Cox's 1995 book, *Fire From Heaven*. Yet, while Betty Lou does not represent a fair portrait of the five hundred million Pentecostals and Charismatics worshipping across the globe in the twenty-first century, just as I argue in chapter one, her individual story does lend

---

[2] Anderson, *An Introduction to Pentecostalism*, p. 1.

[3] Agnes Ozman LaBerge received the baptism in the Holy Spirit in 1901, but many cite the 1906 revivals on Azusa Street as the beginning of American Pentecostalism since they had a wide-spread effect over the three years they ran. People from all over the United States visited Azusa Street and were changed by it. Few were affected by the 1901 events, except in that they led to the 1906 revival because Seymour was influenced by Parham. Thus, the discrepancy. However, this explanation is more complex than just numbers. Of course, there are also the historical precedents described in Vinson Synan's *The Old-Time Power* linking the sanctification and baptism experiences to historical figures since the time of Martin Luther, as well as finding precedent for Pentecostalism in the Cane Ridge Awakening in Kentucky in 1800, and in the 1867 Vineland camp meeting in New Jersey (30, 37). On an even broader scale, today, Pentecostalism is spoken of on global terms with global precedents. These are covered in Allan Anderson's *An Introduction to Pentecostalism* and in Synan's *The Century of the Holy Spirit*, as well as recent issues of *Pneuma*.

[4] Synan, *The Century of the Holy Spirit*, pp. 1-2.

[5] Synan, *The Century of the Holy Spirit*, p. 2.

us something to help us understand the larger rhetorical tradition of early and mid-twentieth century Pentecostal preachers.

In the book, Cox presents Betty Lou as the epitome of the stereotypical Pentecostal woman preacher. She is poor, uneducated, unsophisticated, and seems to take a somewhat fundamentalist approach to her faith except that she feels that the authority of Scripture may be superseded by divine revelation since that is her justification for being a preacher. Betty Lou is from an extremely conservative town south of Charleston, West Virginia, and her sermon is transcribed in Cox's text, along with a description of her every breath and her every motion to illustrate her dramatic and barely believable call story. Through his cold descriptions, Cox reduces Betty Lou to little more than a specimen under his microscope with all of the connotations of power and the portrayal of 'normal' versus 'abnormal' that such a metaphor provides. However, what we can take from Cox's description is that her call story fits into a 'call-refusal motif' that characterizes the call stories of many women preachers.[6] Cox finds biblical precedents for this paradigm such as when Moses first refused to lead his people out of Egypt and when Jonah first refused to go preach to Nineveh.[7] The motif fits some Oklahomans' stories as well.

Like Cox, folklorist Elaine Lawless uses rural women preachers to characterize Pentecostal preachers in *Handmaidens of the Lord*. She describes the Pentecostal's legalistic dress codes and thereby gives us a picture of a group of backward, somewhat isolated women in Missouri refusing to wear make-up or cut their hair. Lawless supports the stereotype that Pentecostal women preachers are uneducated fundamentalists who nevertheless find a way to subvert the hierarchy and preach while ironically reinforcing the hierarchy itself. She writes, 'It is difficult to ascertain why women can hold prime leadership roles in this religion that takes the Bible very literally and which openly supports a male-dominated hierarchy'.[8] The women who do preach, she writes, get their call directly from God, al-

---

[6] Harvey Cox, *Fire From Heaven: The Rise of Pentecostal Spirituality and the Reshaping of Religion in the Twenty-first Century* (Cambridge, MA: Da Capo Press, 1995), p. 130.

[7] Cox, *Fire From Heaven*, pp. 130-32.

[8] Elaine J. Lawless, *Handmaidens of the Lord: Pentecostal Women Preachers and Traditional Religion* (Philadelphia: University of Pennsylvania Press, 1988), p. 42.

though all of these call stories exhibit the 'call-refusal motif' Cox describes.[9] Like Cox, in her chapter on Pentecostal women preachers Mary McClintock Fulkerson carries the stereotype forward when she writes that she is using interviews of 'backward, uncultured, and primitive mountain folk' from the 1930s and 40s.[10]

So what were IPHC Pentecostal women preachers like in the late nineteenth and early twentieth centuries? How far had they come by the 30s and 40s? The stereotypes Cox and Fulkerson share ring true, with some areas for qualification, in the autobiographies and biographies of early IPHC preachers. However, while it is also fair to describe them as poor and as unsophisticated, rural folk, it is also fair to point out that a majority of settlers in the west would fit the same description, just as McClintock does. Even so the simplicity of the stereotype is challenged by the IPHC's history. For example, Bishop/Superintendent J.H. King had a coveted college education. In fact, King describes his international travels in his autobiography, something few people in the late nineteenth and early twentieth centuries had the luxury to experience. Others in the denomination had varying levels of education and experience that defy the simplicity of the stereotypical paradigm as well. As their stories unfold, the stereotype of the Pentecostal preacher will be complicated in light of real experiences, and it will be undermined by a look at the lives of late twentieth/early twenty-first century women preachers who are anything but poor, uneducated, or legalistic.

Oklahoma's Important Role in IPHC History

Though the IPHC began in North Carolina and spread, my focus is on the development of the Pentecostal Holiness and the Fire-Baptized denominations in Oklahoma for several reasons. Besides the fact that I am a native Oklahoman and hold deep ties to the state, it is the current location of the IPHC headquarters or Resource Development Center, the Southwestern College of Christian Ministries, and the place where other colleges, such as King's College, tried and failed.[11] Also, IPHC historian Joseph Campbell wrote

---

[9] Lawless, *Handmaidens of the Lord*, p. 44.
[10] Mary McClintock Fulkerson, *Changing the Subject: Women's Discourses and Feminist Theology* (Minneapolis: Fortress Press, 1994), p. 239.
[11] Synan, *Old Time Power*, p. 183.

that the Oklahoma Conference was 'indirectly responsible for about all of the work in the West', an opinion that Synan echoes in his later history.[12] Synan validates Campbell's claim when he describes the exit of 'Okies' during the depression and Dust Bowl years.[13] Some of these Pentecostals left and took their doctrine with them.

Oklahoma is also notable historically for several other reasons. In Harold Paul's biography of Dan Muse we learn that the first Sunday School Convention in the IPHC was held in April of 1920 in Oklahoma City.[14] The year before, Mrs. Addie Muse had served on a Sunday School Committee that recommended the organization of a conference wide Sunday School association.[15] Harold Hunter notes that 'the 1911 merger was between the IPHC located primarily in North Carolina and the much larger Fire-Baptized Holiness Association (FBHA)' and this merger 'spread across the USA and beyond', but Irwin, the founder of the FBHA, 'got his 1895 fire baptism in Indian Territory. In 1906, he opened the first FBHA in Iowa then opened one in El Reno, Oklahoma the following year. In 1906, a FBH congregation in Lamont, OK accepted the Azusa message when Cook came to them directly from Azusa'. This 'predates the revival in Dunn, North Carolina'.[16]

Synan also tells us that Agnes Ozman LaBerge joined the Oklahoma Convention as a minister in 1909. She was noted for being the first to provide evidence of Charles Parham's doctrine that the baptism of the Holy Spirit was evident when a person spoke in tongues. Also notable about Oklahoma is that in 1972 the first African-American congregation to be an official part of the church since 1913 was a local church in Altus, Oklahoma. In addition, the most famous preacher to ever come out of the IPHC was Oral Roberts, a 'young evangelist in the East Oklahoma Conference'. He rose to fame during the 1950s and was attracting over 10,000 people at a time to his healing crusades. By 1965 Roberts was known around the world and was set to open Oral Roberts University in

---

[12] Joseph Campbell, *The Pentecostal Holiness Church, 1898-1948* (Franklin Springs, GA: The Publishing House of the Pentecostal Holiness Church, 1951), p. 215. Synan, *Old Time Power*, p. 178.

[13] Synan, *Old Time Power*, pp. 196-97.

[14] Harold Paul, *From Printer's Devil to Bishop* (Franklin Springs, GA: Advocate Press, 1976), p. 43.

[15] Paul, *From Printer's Devil to Bishop*, p. 37.

[16] Personal correspondence from Harold Hunter, May 25, 2010.

Tulsa, Oklahoma. Native Oklahoman and General Secretary for the IPHC, R.O. Corvin was selected to be the head of ORU's Theology Department. Vinson Synan's father participated in the dedication ceremonies for ORU alongside the famous Billy Graham. Unfortunately, Roberts left the IPHC denomination in 1968 to join the United Methodist Church.[17] These are a few of the reasons Oklahoma has significance and a rightful place in the IPHC history books. More than that, an 'Oklahoman' ethos generated by a relationship between the land and its people can tell us much about how ethos is generated by those who occupy other contexts if readers use the descriptions and experiences to draw parallels out of their own lives as I did.

Outlaws and Cowboys

As a place of rich history, Oklahoma defies categorization. We are not really 'southern', though one can see strains of it. We are not really 'Midwestern' either, at least according to my experiences with Midwesterners. Classified as a Southwestern state, I would argue that Oklahoma is a place that breathes the same sort of air as Texas, but with its heavy Native American influence as opposed to the Hispanic influence in Tucson, it is also a place all unto itself. In a recent car trip, my father summed it up perfectly: 'Oklahoma is just a bunch of cowboys trying to be sophisticated. But they aren't there yet'. Indeed, with its rich history as Native American Territory, and with the infusion of hearty, pioneer settlers who participated in its most famous land run in 1889, Oklahoma's character defies simplistic categorization. It is something of an 'other' among the lower forty-eight.

If ethos can be imagined as a way to build identification with a particular sort of reader and if ethos can be thought of as a tool of transformation and as a means of exhibiting charisma, then understanding what kinds of bridges needed to be built to convert Oklahomans is worth addressing. For one, audience plays a significant role in the ideas associated with generative ethos, as outlined in chapter one.

---

[17] Synan, *Old Time Power*, pp. 133-267.

We get a picture of Oklahomans in a 'history' left to us by a Nazarene preacher. Late nineteenth/early twentieth century preacher and self-proclaimed historian C.B. Jernigan wrote that in 1897 Native American Territory was 'owned, but unallotted by the Indians', leased mostly to 'cattle men' and owned by farmers living in its rich valleys.[18] These people lived in dugouts and log cabins. In general, 'the inhabitants were Indians, cowboys, and many desperate characters who had gone there to escape the law in other states'. According to Jernigan, the soon-to-be-converts 'spent their Sundays in drinking "chock", a native beer manufactured by the Choctaw Indians, and in gambling and carousing'. As a Pentecostal Nazarene, Jernigan claimed that it took a 'preach or burn' spirit to reach these people and a 'pioneer spirit' that had little to do with settling the land and everything to do with spreading charismatic Pentecostalism.[19]

Jernigan also describes the mentality of the Native Americans who inhabited Oklahoma in the early twentieth century. He criticizes them for not wanting to settle down or farm and described them as going about 'in droves mostly' living in 'cloth tents' and 'houses made of weeds well tied together'.[20] He also writes:

> The Indian has a high ideal of religion, that will radically change and make him new all over. They think that when God saves a man he must give up his tobacco, pipe, Mescal bean, and whisky. At a camp meeting held at the Ponca Indian agency especially for the Indians, in company with Rev. I.G. Martin, in 1910, a great many Indians came and camped. We saw thirty Indians at the altar, praying in Ponca language and weeping with broken hearts over their sins. Many were really saved. At the close of the meeting Brother Martin called a council of the leaders of the tribe to know if they desired the continuation of the Nazarene mission among them. All the old braves were asked to speak. White Eagle, the last chief of his tribe, who was known among them as

---

[18] C.B. Jernigan, *Pioneer Days of the Holiness Movement in the Southwest* (reprinted by Charles Edwin Jones, 2002; Kansas City, MO: Pentecostal Nazarene Publishing House, 1919), p. 54.

[19] Jernigan, *Pioneer Days*, p. 59. The designation 'Pentecostal' was pre-Azusa Street, and was removed after the Nazarenes rejected the theology of Azusa Street.

[20] Jernigan, *Pioneer Days*, p. 128.

their silver-tongued orator, arose and spoke through an inter-
preter. He said, 'When I was a baby they took me to a priest who
sprinkled water on my head, and told my mother that I was a
Christian, but it did not touch my heart. Same bad heart. The
government takes our children and makes them learn from
book. They go to the Methodist mission; learn to sing good; listen to smart man talk; still same bad Indian. They go to Nazarene meeting; get on their knees, cry and pray to God till face
shines; they go home, read a Bible, pray. No more eat Mescal
bean; no more drink whisky. No more smoke pipe. No more
steal. Come on Nazarenes'.

In Jernigan's description of the ideal missionary or evangelist for
the young state, he says that not only was the state full of outlaws
and cowboys, but few had ever even heard the gospel. 'It was indeed a very needy field, and ripe for the sickle of the pioneer who
dared trust God and go without the promise of a cent for remu-
neration, and expect to get his reward at the end of the race'.[21]

The audiences faced by early IPHC preachers became a part of
the ethos they created in order to achieve their goals—winning
souls and providing opportunities for Holy Spirit baptisms, for example. Mikhail Bahktin writes that 'understanding and response are
dialectically merged and mutually condition each other; one is impossible without the other'.[22] Thus, describing the audience helps to
demonstrate how it determined the ethos of the writer/preacher
because ethos does not emerge in a vacuum. The 'language' of a
group emerges within those social and historical contexts that define it or provide places for resistance. In fact, the idea that 'language' is 'unitary' is only true when it is thought of as an 'abstract
grammatical system of normative forms, taken in isolation from the
concrete, ideological conceptualizations that fill it, and in isolation
from the uninterrupted process of historical becoming that is characteristic of all language'.[23] Thus, the 'language' of the IPHC
preachers was partially formed by their desire to bridge what di-
vided them from the unsaved Oklahomans for whom they cared so

---

[21] Jernigan, *Pioneer Days*, p. 128.
[22] M.M. Bakhtin, *The Dialogic Imagination* (ed. Michael Holquist; trans. Caryl
Emerson and Michael Holquist; Austin: University of Texas Press, 1990), p. 282.
[23] Bakhtin, *The Dialogic Imagination*, p. 288.

deeply, even though those audiences were a very real threat to the well being of these preachers.

Both IPHC preacher Robert Rex and IPHC biographer Harold Paul echo Jernigan in their own descriptions of Oklahoma's people when they write that Oklahoma was a repository for many unlawful people who came to the unsettled west in order to escape the law, particularly after the Civil War.[24] These people, it was felt, needed religion to help them monitor their own behavior because the law was not established enough to help them or to protect them from others. Though early IPHC doctrines were more radically enforced and argued for than they would be in later days, it is not just because of the radical nature of the religion itself; it is an indication of how the preacher must build ethos with an audience that knew a life regulated more by their own decision to be 'good' than by a community's organized enforcement of the 'good'.

In Harold Paul's biography of former Bishop Dan Muse, he describes the liquor, gambling, and prostitution rackets that plagued Oklahoma City in the early 20th-century.[25] He quotes Muse, who wrote:

> The early preachers and workers met with determined opposition from many religionists and endured much suffering and many privations. Persecution was rife. Many were rocked [had rocks thrown at them] and had eggs thrown at them. Others met up with red pepper being thrown in the straw to bring discomfort to the worshippers. Tents were slashed, and doors were locked on them. Some were threatened with death by hanging, and others were arrested and spent a night or so in jail.[26]

Paul also tells us that Muse slept with a six-gun 'under the pillow just in case of trouble' and very wisely ignored the 'moonshiners' while walking to and from preaching appointments through the densely forested Oklahoma countryside, preferring prayer to confrontation.[27] 'His job was to preach, and he stuck strictly to his own

---

[24] Robert Rex, *I Was Compelled by Love: People Called Me 'Mr. Evangelism'* (Franklin Springs, GA: Advocate, 1982), p. 7; Paul, *From Printer's Devil to Bishop*, pp. 11-15.

[25] Paul, *From Printer's Devil to Bishop*, pp. 11-12.

[26] Paul, *From Printer's Devil to Bishop*, p. 20.

[27] Paul, *From Printer's Devil to Bishop*, pp. 21, 30.

business', Paul writes. The implication is, of course, that Muse's safety depended on such an attitude.

Late nineteenth and early twentieth-century Oklahomans were indeed threatening. Lucy Hargis describes a time when she and her husband had fasted and prayed all day and still did not get a message to preach, but preached anyway.[28] However, 'as his feet hit the pulpit the power came down and he [Lee] preached mightily under the anointing and stepped out on the altar to make the altar call'. People ran to the altar and after the service, a new convert told Lee that he and some of his friends had planned to hang him at that very service, but 'when we came up to the arbor a rainbow of fire settled down upon it and we saw a ball of fire shoot through the arbor and we were afraid and I'm glad God has saved my soul tonight'.

It is clear that the potential converts of Oklahoma in its early years of statehood, whether they were a part of the growing cities or countryside towns, were a difficult group to reach and required a strong, passionate message in order to feel the need for change. The ethos generated from these tough potential converts resulted in a characterization of early and middle IPHC preachers as people willing to risks their lives at most and their comfort at least in order to convey their message. Because the crowds were difficult and the social bonds of law enforcement were loose, the ethos of the Pentecostal preacher had to convey some elements of bravado, some indications of physical as well as spiritual strength, and perhaps even some deep love or regard made evident through their sincerity that made the potential converts abandon a decision to oppose them and decide, instead, to join a group they formerly found suspicious. Identification, then, meant understanding their audience and appealing to them through pathos as well as ethos in order to achieve persuasion.

In addition to the very real dangers and difficulties of being a Pentecostal preacher in Oklahoma, whether you were man or woman, contemporary historian Susan Peterson describes the poverty and hardship for evangelists in her chapter, 'Patient, Useful Servants: Women Missionaries in Indian Territory'. The main impe-

---

[28] Lucy Hargis, unpublished letter (on file at Bethany, OK: IPHC Archives, 1975), pp. 1-35 (20).

tus for women to enter Native American Territory in the late nine-teenth/early twentieth centuries was as missionaries and in response to the need for school teachers, she reveals.[29] Not only was the prospect of work there—albeit low paid—but the motivation to go was in response to sermons encouraging missionaries to 'bring light to "heathens" all over the world'. On the one hand, the Native Americans were much closer than the foreign countries often mentioned. On the other hand, Peterson relates some now-forgotten reasons why Native Americans were not evangelized more. For example, many had refused to accept Christianity, and then there was a popular belief that the Native Americans were dying off because of God's divine plan.[30] Even so these teachers/missionaries went with a sense of adventure and hope to what would be the state of Oklahoma as of 1907.

Unfortunately, for those who made it there to serve as teachers and missionaries who were bent on shaping the character of their students, 'primitive dwellings and unpredictable weather' awaited.[31] Worse was the prevalence of disease and the amount of work left to be accomplished by those who survived.[32] Besides these obstacles, women faced 'loneliness, monotony, and isolation'. Peterson reports that many diaries reflect the deep sense of boredom experienced in a place originally imagined to be of such great adventure.[33]

In contrast, one of the IPHC's first female evangelists, Dollie York, certainly was not plagued with boredom. Instead, her husband Dan tells their story in a short autobiography left to us called 'Life Events of Dan and Dollie York', and through his words we get a glimpse of his 'dark, sun-burned woman with black keen eyes who saw everything as it was'.[34] And, unlike the women Peterson describes, the Yorks were not alone.

---

[29] Susan Peterson, 'Patient, Useful Servants: Women Missionaries in Indian Territory', in Melvena K. Thurman (ed.), *Women in Oklahoma: A Century of Change* (Oklahoma City: Oklahoma Historical Society, 1982), pp. 106-107.

[30] Peterson, 'Patient, Useful Servants', p. 108.

[31] Peterson, 'Patient, Useful Servants', p. 113.

[32] Peterson, 'Patient, Useful Servants', p. 114.

[33] Peterson, 'Patient, Useful Servants', p. 114.

[34] Dan York, *Life Events of Dan and Dollie York* (Oklahoma City: Charles Edwin Jones, 2002).

'I Stand in Good Relation to the Earth'[35]

We first see Oklahoma itself, not just its people, as a force to be dealt with in Dan York's story. He describes a trip through Native American Territory in 1891 as follows:

> We were overtaken by a snowstorm at Tar Springs, just west of Ardmore, Oklahoma a way. We stopped with a good old Indian Territory man, who had just finished a log cabin 16 x 18 foot, chinked and dobbed, covered with boards and had no ceiling on it ... A storm [came] on and one of those blue blizzards [started] turning to snow. It fell to a depth of 12 inches and water was half a mile away. All 18 of us had to eat and sleep in this cabin for 10 days, but it looked so good to us. It was so cold and the snow covered our bedding while we slept. We also had to hunt game for our eats. Soon we began to hit the rocks and break camp, slipping the oxen across the stream on ice, then all together we slipped the wagon down the bank and across on the ice, as there were no bridges nor any roads to follow.[36]

In the second chapter of his book, Dan goes back a bit to describe his conversion before the trip to Native American Territory in 1891. In 1889, Dan walked three miles to a Methodist church in his 'homemade suit' and no shoes.[37] There he was saved at an altar with his Uncle John York's hand on his head. But a true sense of Oklahoma, as it was back then, can be seen in the warning he received shortly before the move to Native American Territory He was plainly told not to go because he 'could not keep his religion out there'.

Between the weather and the people, Oklahoma's newest inhabitants required a spirit of determination and courage. Dollie York was certainly equal to the challenge. As Dan's story of their lives goes on, we find out that they married in 1898 and ended up in Pauls Valley, Oklahoma in 1903.[38] Dan writes that they leased a farm in Wolf, Native American Territory, in 1904. It was situated

---

35 From Momaday, 'The Delight Song of Tsoai-talee'.
36 York, *Life Events*, p. 2.
37 York, *Life Events*, p. 8.
38 York, *Life Events*, p. 6.

among the Seminoles. 'Some of them would not even meet us in the road', he writes, 'they did not want us in their country'. Not long after they settled, Dan and Dollie were ordained by the Holiness Church of Christ and built themselves a brush arbor to preach under. But they were not to remain affiliated with the church for long.

As unbelievable as it might seem to us today, Dan and Dollie heard about the events of Azusa Street and subsequently believed that it was possible for them to receive the baptism of the Holy Ghost and speak in tongues.[39] They received their 'Pentecost' after two men attended services that were conducted by J.H. King (Superintendent/Bishop in the IPHC) in Lamont, Oklahoma; they then conducted their own service in Beulah, Oklahoma.[40] As schools were built and churches planted in the wave of Pentecostal fire, Dan and Dollie moved about Oklahoma, preaching and sharing their experience of Pentecost. No obstacle to sharing the faith was too great. Dan writes that at one camp meeting, they even had to dig a well.[41] He estimated that '1500 to 2000 were there every night to hear the word' and that '65 fell at the altar' the night Dollie spoke. They heard J.H. King themselves in Stratford, Oklahoma, in 1909 or 1910.[42] Thus the new beliefs and the charisma of rising IPHC leaders and preachers point to the power of ethos in Oklahoma and to the charisma of African-American preacher Seymour on Azusa Street in Los Angeles.

When a muddy Oklahoma river almost took their wagon and soaked all of their belongings in Carr, Oklahoma, the very real difficulty of the place was made evident.[43] Fortunately, they were helped out of the river and left on its banks. The next day they crossed the Canadian River with the help of another man. Dan writes, 'We finally got across, with the water jumping over the horses' hips in the wagon bed'. Dan's next statement reveals how his ethos was enmeshed with place, with God, and with a determination to evangelize Oklahoma: 'We were so glad our God was with us. This is the God you cannot drown out'.

---

[39] York, *Life Events*, p. 7.
[40] York, *Life Events*, p. 8.
[41] York, *Life Events*, p. 10.
[42] York, *Life Events*, p. 11.
[43] York, *Life Events*, p. 13.

Often sick, tired, hungry, or wet, Dan and Dollie York bravely preached in the streets and in the Oklahoma woods, drawing people to participate in the baptism of the Holy Spirit, although it was hotly opposed by many who would not hesitate to do them violence. Indeed, more than one physical confrontation was recorded by Dan, but what stands out is the passion with which Dan and Dollie spread Pentecostalism without any of the social, religious, or even governmental structures in place that so many of us now rely upon to do our work. Such bravery required much more commitment than we see today. Certainly Oklahoma's people and landscape required them to value their lives and possessions in a much different way than today. Its inhabitants provided IPHC preachers with challenges, but so did the place itself. But these preachers simply adapted their beliefs to fit the place, much like I did, and integrated their experiences of God into the Christian ethos formed on its bright, red clay.

Oklahoma's Beauty

Oklahoma itself—the landscape, the weather, and the economic structure that forced so many early IPHC preachers to live off the land at times, to go without food at other times, to make their journeys on foot, to preach in brush arbors when they had no tent, and to value the hospitality of those who could offer them little more than a roof for a night—was still a place of beauty, and it shaped the spiritual identities of its occupants. The daughter of former Bishop Dan Muse, IPHC member Margaret Muse Oden describes it in her memoirs (published in 1955) as follows:

> Here amid woods thick with blackjacks, pastures ablaze with early spring blossoms, cedar trees strong and rugged with their many years of growth, orchards loaded with blossoms, then transformed into abundant fruitage, plowed fields yielding a harvest of vegetables or of golden grain, they followed a simple pattern of life—but, oh, so rich in the contentment of living close to God's creation—enhanced with the peace flowing

through the souls of those responding to the ministry of the Bishop.[44]

And, while Grace Hope Curtis remembers not having air conditioning in the summer or heat in her car as she drove through the snow to preach a revival, having to use gaslights or lanterns instead of electric, and having to battle with bugs attracted to the lights while she preached, even she admits Oklahoma was not always her a place of difficulty.[45] She describes a 'wonderful bedroom' she had in Fairfax, Oklahoma, where she 'slept out under the stars in a lady's fenced backyard'.[46] Even so, Oklahoma's winter weather added to the pain she felt when she was away from her family. She describes crying and praying in the 'wee hours' of the night on the 'bare cold floor' long after the 'wood fires would go out'.[47] Perhaps if ethos can be imagined as a tool to transform the audience, it can also be imagined as a tool to transform the rhetors whose lives and attitudes must be altered by the beauty and hardships of the place where identity is enacted.

Oklahoma's Native Americans and Pioneers

Ethos is collective because we are influenced by those around us, even if our inner selves are not completely determined by them. We move by choice, by relationship, by perception, by identification, and by self-construction. We are shaped by place, by community, and for the Christian, by the work of the Spirit. Unique to Oklahomans, perhaps, is the fact that our state was originally the rightful home of several Native American tribes. Thus, ties to Oklahoma's own 'ethos' can be seen in the explicit claims to Native American heritage made by two Oklahoma preachers I studied, Grace Hope Curtis and Robert L. Rex. Essentially, claiming to have Native American blood ties meant they were essentially claiming the land in Oklahoma even though, as Historian Richard White tells us, 'the

---

[44] Margaret Muse Oden, *Steps to the Sun* (Franklin Springs, GA: The Publishing House of The Pentecostal Holiness Church, 1955), p. 45.

[45] Grace Hope Curtis, *Pioneer Woman for Christ: The Life and Ministry of Grace Hope Curtis* (Tulsa, OK: Johnnie Hope & Associates, 1978), pp. 18-26.

[46] Curtis, *Pioneer Woman for Christ*, p. 23.

[47] Curtis, *Pioneer Woman for Christ*, p. 19.

idea of a permanent Indian country died early in its childhood' as Oklahoma 'fell victim to American expansionism'.[48]

In the early years of Oklahoma's statehood, in the 'home of the Red Man', it was shameful to be a Native American, but by the time Curtis' autobiography was published in the late 70s, it was a point of pride. She tells us on the first page that her mother was 'French on her father's side' and Cherokee on her mother's side.[49] As proof, she writes that her 'grandmother's picture as a young girl looked like an Indian Princess—very beautiful'. She then intersperses her early childhood history with references to her 'Indian blood'. She says that because she was the baby, her family thought she was the 'greatest little papoose in the whole territory'. When she describes how she and her siblings hid whenever people came out to their remote farm in Oklahoma which was still Native American Territory at the time, she says, 'We were not afraid of coyotes or wild bulls, but people were something else! We didn't want to be around them. I guess our Indian blood was showing!'[50] Then, she illustrates her difference from 'real' Native Americans when she chronicles a meeting between a woman and her father. Riding up on her horse, she came to ask for fire or a lit coal to be put in her shovel. Her father gave her matches instead. Curtis recalls that the Native American woman called them 'the white man's fire at the end of a stick'.

A similar pride as well as distance in his Native American bloodlines can be seen in my grandfather's autobiography published during the same decade. Although my grandfather, IPHC preacher Robert Rex, was more English than anything else—with blonde, curly hair in his youth, white skin, and bright blue eyes—he includes mention of his Native American roots on the first page of his autobiography. His great-grandmother was Cherokee and might have come over on the Trail of Tears, he tells us.[51] He didn't know her name—only that she was referred to as 'the little maiden with the withered hand'.

It is ironic that my grandfather includes his own Native American bloodlines but not my grandmother's. My grandmother was a

---

[48] Richard White, *It's Your Misfortune and None of My Own: A New History of the American West* (Norman, OK: University of Oklahoma Press, 1993), p. 89.

[49] Curtis, *Pioneer Woman for Christ*, p. 9.

[50] Curtis, *Pioneer Woman for Christ*, p. 10.

[51] Rex, *I Was Compelled by Love*, p. 1.

tiny, black-haired woman with distinctive Native American features and dark brown eyes. She was clearly tied to Oklahoma's ethnic heritage though she was born in Rising Star, Texas, in 1907, the same year Oklahoma achieved statehood; but her life was as a white woman. She did not have the language or the customs of her Cherokee ancestors. However, my mother says that grandma would tell her that her great-grandmother was full-blood Cherokee and because of that bloodline, grandma had decided that since God had put a love for bright colors in Native Americans, she and mom did not have to abide by holiness standards of the day that called for drab colors and plain dress like other Pentecostals did.

The role of ethos in references to their Native American bloodlines in the autobiographies of Curtis and Rex might be simply construed as bridge-building, but a closer look reveals that Curtis often felt called to minister to Native Americans in Oklahoma. Preaching to them in schoolhouses and understanding the work was both dangerous and unpaid, but her love for Oklahoma's people perhaps stemmed from her identification with them. For Rex, references to his Native American bloodlines were both a claim to the land and to a place in history. A history-buff, the first chapter of his autobiography is full of Oklahoma's history and how he saw his life as embedded in Oklahoma's master narrative.

Another focus for both Rex and Curtis was on their identity as pioneers, both as early IPHC preachers and as early settlers in Oklahoma. The 'pioneer' ethos communicated the right mix of Americanism and determination needed to appeal to the potential converts. Evidence of their desire to construct themselves as pioneers can be seen by the covers they chose for their autobiographies. Curtis' autobiography, titled *Pioneer Woman for Christ,* features a statue in Ponca City, Oklahoma, called 'The Pioneer Woman'. The woman is striding forward, in long dress, bonnet, a bag, and tie-up boots, holding the hand of a young boy, perhaps seven or eight years old. The woman's expression is unsmiling, but unworried. The boy next to her looks like he has to work hard at keeping up with her long, sure strides. The life-sized sculpture communicates the woman's confidence, leadership, and perhaps a sense of her capability. On the back of Curtis' book, she tells us that the statue is by an English sculptor, Bryant Baker, and was dedicated on April 22, 1930, in Ponca City, Oklahoma, on the anniversary of the first run for land in Oklahoma. Visitors to Oklahoma can drive out to Ponca City's Pioneer Woman Museum to see it for themselves even today.

Robert Rex's cover depicts a man driving a horse-drawn wagon down a tree-lined lane past an old tin or wooden building. The cover is a yellow and dark brown two-toned drawing, meant to symbolize the author and his transitory place within the church and American history. Both Curtis and Rex draw upon the pioneer ethos in order to describe the way they moved from farm life to city life, from early preaching in a loosely established denomination to preaching within a firmly established denomination. The pioneer epitaph is their chosen context for their life and work, and the connotation is one of heroic fortitude and faith in the midst of a century of people trying to find their way toward stability amidst growing industrialization and its accompanying hazards. Again, Rex saw himself as a part of Oklahoma itself, and he conscientiously mapped his own history into the history of Oklahoma, localizing his story through a history of the county where he grew up and contextualizing his story through references to historical events that affected the nation as a whole.

The pioneer ethos ran throughout the early and middle twentieth century characterizations of IPHC preachers and connoted a sense of strength and determination for those able to construct a church in sparsely populated areas, with no money, no buildings, and little denominational support. Rex and Curtis incorporated a literal rendition of the pioneer ethos in their autobiographies, but this type of ethos does not supersede their role as pioneer preachers, armed with a new type of faith to offer to an unpredictable audience.

Conclusion

Truly, Oklahoma itself brought out an element of the ethos that characterizes many early IPHC preachers: hard-core determination fueled by faith. In a handwritten letter kept in the IPHC Archives, preacher Lucy Hargis describes how she and her husband had both given up their jobs and gone 'north' by train with a nursing baby simply because they felt that God wanted them to go.[52] They ran out of money, except for a dollar and some change, and had to stay

---

[52] Hargis, unpublished letter, pp. 11-12.

in the McAlester, Oklahoma, train station two days before they met a man. 'Brother' Stevens, who said he was waiting on a preacher to come by train to preach in a revival, mysteriously arrived at that same station and began talking with the Hargises.[53] The preacher Brother Stevens was waiting on never came, so the Hargises left with him. As another young man drove the group away from the station, Brother Stevens played his guitar and they all sang. Lucy felt that God had blessed them as they 'forgot our empty stomachs and our hungry body and our hardships' in the joy of the songs and of God's rescue from the train station.

Hard-core determination fueled by faith is evident in the continuation of the story. Robert Rex picks up where Lucy leaves off. During the next six to eight weeks, the Hargises held a revival in Caddo that drew increasing amounts of attention because of the 'new' doctrine he was preaching—baptism in the Holy Spirit.[54] During that time my great-grandfather became a Christian by Lee Hargis' invitation, and when opposition grew to the teaching and violence was threatened, 'some of the businessmen in town told the opposition group that if Rev. Hargis could get a man like Mr. Rex saved, he could stay and talk in tongues all he wanted'.[55] As the revival progressed, Lee Hargis put out three altars every night: 'one for those seeking to be saved, another for those who wanted to be sanctified, and one for those seeking to be filled with the Holy Spirit'.[56] Thus, the decision made by the Hargises to just get on a train and 'go North' defied logic, but the successful revival that ensued would serve as proof that faith and determination are rewarded. Indeed, Pentecostalism in Oklahoma was and still is something unique.

In conclusion, evidence of ethos in the autobiographies of IPHC preachers such as the Yorks, Curtis, Rex, and the Hargises is evidence that Oklahoma itself played a major role in who they were, in how they experienced their lives and faith, and in how that ethos was co-generated with the realities of their 'outlaw' and 'Indian' audiences just as much as it was with the excitement of the new doctrine, referred to as the baptism in the Holy Spirit. Though it is

---

[53] Hargis, unpublished letter, p. 12.
[54] Rex, *I Was Compelled by Love*, p. 25.
[55] Rex, *I Was Compelled by Love*, p. 29.
[56] Rex, *I Was Compelled by Love*, p. 27.

not as easy to see, the type of determined ethos projected in the autobiographies was a tool of effective transformation for audiences predisposed to be hostile to the Pentecostal faith and message. They legacy of this ethos lives on in the lives of their children today.

3

OUR INHERITANCE

These commandments I give you today are to be upon your hearts. Impress them on your children. Talk about them when you sit at home and when you walk along the road, when you lie down and when you get up. Tie them as symbols on your hands and bind them to your foreheads. Write them on the doorframes of your houses and on your gates (Deut. 6.6-9).

Our inheritances are handed down to us from our parents, from their parents, and from theirs, but also from the denominations that give us life and community. Just as ancient Israel saw herself as a community before God, so do Pentecostals. Our individual lives, our local churches, our denominations, and our affiliations with Pentecostalism as it is written largely on the pages of world history, form a community before God. To understand Pentecostalism as a collective ethos that is incorporated into the lives of the women preachers I studied, the spiritual heritage claimed by Pentecostals must be explored, particularly as it affects the perception of women in the church.

It is helpful to understand that Pentecostalism itself is a broad, descriptive term that describes members from a wide range of denominations. In fact, Synan's book, *The Century of the Holy Spirit: 100 Years of Pentecostal and Charismatic Renewal, 1901-2001*, includes chapters written by different scholars who present groups within the broad history of Pentecostalism, including a chapter describing the most influential Pentecostal women preachers.

Dr. Susan Hyatt's chapter on these influential Pentecostal women preachers includes a broad historical view of women preachers and incorporates even non-Pentecostals such as the Quaker Margaret Fell, the Methodist Phoebe Palmer, Catherine Mumford Booth of the Salvation Army, the Quaker Hannah Whitall Smith who worked closely with Frances Willard of the Woman's Christian Temperance Union for women's suffrage, and others who are directly responsible for opening the way for women who came after them.[1] Thus Hyatt puts the work of Pentecostals into a larger historical context that sets the stage for us to understand the battles that had already been fought and won by the time late nineteenth and early twentieth-century women took their places behind the pulpit.

Hyatt also describes some of the major doctrines supporting women's equality within the church. Three central biblical themes are used by Pentecostal women preachers. These include:

- the 'theme of biblical equality' based upon Gal. 3.28, where Paul describes all Christians as equals,
- the 'redemption argument' based upon the idea that Christ redeemed woman from the Garden of Eden curse with his death and resurrection, and
- the 'Pentecostal theme for biblical equality' based upon Joel 2.28 (quoted in Acts 2.17-18), which states that the Holy Spirit will be poured out on both men and women in the last days.[2]

While others who argued for a woman's right to preach privileged other scriptures, these three themes and scriptures are the true basis from which Pentecostals past and present defend a woman's right to preach.

Making Connections

Our inheritance is more than a history of challenges, of victories, of defeats. It is an inheritance of community. My mother, daughter of IPHC preacher and former Director of World Missions, Robert Rex, was recently invited to participate in a prayer walk for a church Rex used to pastor. The daughter of two former preachers, Lee and Lucy Hargis, was also invited. Former members of the church were invited as well. Together, forming a spiritual bond to the past as it lived through the faith of those living in the present, the prayers

---

[1] Susan Hyatt, 'Spirit Filled Women', in Synan (ed.), *The Century of the Holy Spirit*, pp. 233-64 (234-40).

[2] Hyatt, 'Spirit Filled Women', p. 238.

were made. It is just one example of how the spiritual heritage of those I've written about in this book live on in the hearts of those alive today. It is a precious heritage, but the value of it is misunderstood by outsiders.

Last summer, I sat in a committee meeting listening to an informal speech by one of the committee members about how she had chosen to attend an Episcopalian church in our town. The church's beliefs aligned with both her political and religious beliefs. Her purpose in sharing the reasons for being a part of that church was to communicate to me that I had options other than the Pentecostal one I attend. Although our church is the only one in Farmville that has both Caucasian and African-American members, its alignment with conservative Christianity—and by extension, Republican politics—was distasteful to her. Although I understand that not all Pentecostals are Republicans, nor are all conservatives, this is a common assumption. As I listened to her, somewhat amused and somewhat irritated, I wondered if she would have made the same speech had I been Jewish? Or Muslim? My denomination is only about 112 years old, but it is just as much a part of me as these other people of faith.

Yet I understand that many no longer see conservativism or Pentecostalism as relevant for the twenty-first century; and in the push for new politics, the push for new religion can be felt as well. As I thought over some of these things in the summer of 2009, I decided to ask if the current Bishop of the IPHC might agree to speak to some of these issues and explain the relevance of Pentecostalism to Christians today.

Bishop James Leggett

Thus, in July of 2009 I was fortunate to have the opportunity to interview James Leggett. At the time of the interview, Bishop Leggett was completing his twelfth year as Bishop.[3] After his retirement last summer, he became the President of Holmes Bible College, 'the oldest Bible College in the United States'. Mr. Leggett's history with the IPHC is long. He was

---

[3] This is according to LaDonna Scott, 'Biography of Bishop James Leggett' (Unpublished interview, June 2006). Scott was Leggett's Administrative Assistant.

a member of the North Carolina Conference of the IPHC where he served as pastor for 24 years. He was elected as Conference Superintendent in 1986. During his superintendency, he was elected to the position of Assistant General Superintendent for the denomination. In 1993, he was elected Vice Chairman of the denomination. From 1989 to 1997, his portfolio included Executive Director of Evangelism USA and President of the Extension Loan Fund.[4]

What is most interesting about Bishop Leggett is that he is part of many influential Christian organizations and is now leader of the Pentecostal World Fellowship. According to his biography, he has

> served as co-chairperson of the Pentecostal/Charismatic Churches of North America (PCCNA) and currently serves on the board of directors. He serves on the board of directors for the National Association of Evangelicals, is a member of Mission America, American Society for Church Growth, the International Charismatic Consultation Advisory Council (ICC), the Christian Churches Together (CCT), and the Religious Alliance Against Pornography (RAAP).[5]

Clearly, Bishop Leggett has an understanding of the religious landscape that few of us will ever glimpse.

In addition to his experience holding the highest positions, not only in the IPHC but also in the national and international organizations listed above, Bishop Leggett is highly educated. In 1988 he was awarded a Doctor of Divinity from Holmes Bible College.

Bishop Leggett's wife has had a successful ministry as well. She was the general director of the Ministers' Wives Fellowship at the time of the interview, and she previously served as vice president of the General Women's Ministries for about eight years.

In the interview that follows, Bishop Leggett speaks on what it means to be Pentecostal in the twenty-first century. He shares his views on women's leadership and on how his wife's ministry has impacted his own, all the while providing the perspective of an individual who is clearly an important part of not only what it means

---

[4] Scott, 'Biography'.
[5] Scott, 'Biography'.

to be Pentecostal today, but also what it will mean to be Pentecostal in the years to come.

Interview with Bishop James Leggett[6]

As Bishop of the International Pentecostal Holiness Church and as Chairman of the Pentecostal World Fellowship, what would you say that it means to be 'Pentecostal' in the twenty-first century?

We just celebrated Azusa Street and the IPHC Centennial, and I've probably preached numerous centennial messages in local churches and conferences.

It is exciting to be Pentecostal in the twenty-first century. From a very small beginning at the turn of the twentieth century, Pentecostalism has become the fastest growing part of the Christian Church. There are more than 600 million Pentecostals in the world. The most explosive growth is in Africa, Asia, and Latin America. The largest churches in the world are now Pentecostal. There are so many open doors for Pentecostals around the world.

We celebrate the wonderful things God has done through Pentecostalism, but we must make a commitment to the future. It is also important that we make sure that we pass Pentecost to the next generation. I am serving on the Holy Spirit Empowerment for the 21st Century Committee. The purpose of the committee is to focus the church on the reality and power of the Holy Spirit for this century. We plan to focus on the main tenets of Pentecostalism and make them relevant to this generation. These truths would be the Holy Spirit Baptism, speaking with tongues, divine healing, the gifts of the Spirit, etc. Oral Roberts feels we must maintain our distinctive of speaking with tongues.

The younger generation calls for a different method of presentation. They still want Pentecost, but they are not hung up on terms. We need to change terms and phrases, but not the core experience. The challenge is to adapt to change with a deep commitment to the baptism of the Holy Spirit, speaking with tongues, and using the fullness of the spiritual gifts.

---

[6] This interview was conducted by telephone on July 8, 2009. Throughout this and subsequent interviews, the questions are italicized and the responses are in plain text.

The Next Generation also wants more authenticity. No more 'show'; they want substance and reality. They want real healings, real miracles, not pretense.

What does 'gender equality' mean to Pentecostals?

It's part of the DNA of the Pentecostal movement. Women were in the forefront of the Azusa revival and they continue to be a major part of Pentecost today. There has been a release of women into ministry because of the Pentecostal movement. There are some Pentecostal churches that license but will not ordain women, but our church ordains women.

There has been a re-emphasis on women in ministry in the IPHC. God promises in Joel 2.28: 'I will pour out my Spirit upon all flesh; your sons and your daughters shall prophesy ... and on my menservants and my maid servants I will pour out my Spirit in those days'.

There are not as many women in leadership as there should be, but there are women in leadership roles in the denomination.

Your wife is a minister and a popular speaker. How has her ministry impacted yours?

My wife was mentored by a Pentecostal pioneer in Norfolk, Virginia. She told Faye she would follow in her footsteps. Mrs. Heddy Edge was her pastor's wife, but she preached numerous times in the church as well as being a sought-after evangelist. Mrs. Edge was a far better preacher than her husband, and she preached much of the time. The congregation would watch to see if she had on her hat because it meant she would preach. In fact, she traveled across country doing revivals and was still holding revivals in her late 70s.

Faye went to Holmes and was granted missions license at the age of sixteen in the Eastern Conference. Our speech teacher at Holmes said to me one day, 'You know your girlfriend is a better speaker than you'. She does communicate well. She spoke at a recent men's meeting in North Carolina. We were told she did a better job than the rest of us.

Most pastors now see ministry as a partnership. Many wives are listed as co-pastors. Faye has also been important to Women's Ministries and to the Minister's Wives Fellowship. She's been a vital part of my ministry and I thank God for her speaking ability and her modeling of the minister's wife as a partner.

In your opinion, why aren't there more women serving in the IPHC, both in the GMC as well as in conference leadership positions?

That still may be the glass ceiling. There aren't as many women in leadership roles, but we have had a conference superintendent who was a woman. Charlene West was Director of Hispanic Ministries, Shirley Spencer is editor of the IPHC Experience, and the head of Human Resources is now a woman. Barbara James served as Director of Win, our prayer ministry. Women do serve on the conference boards, and I believe the number of women in leadership on the conference level will increase.

You serve on the boards of many influential Christian organizations, such as the NAE and CCT, for example. How have you been able to impact these organizations, such as on issues of gender equality, for example?

The Pentecostals were founding members of NAE. As a Pentecostal, I served on the steering committee in the formation of CCT. I now serve as the president of the evangelical/Pentecostal family in CCT. The biggest impact has been in the acceptance of the Pentecostal message. There was a time when Pentecost was looked at with suspicion by many in the church world. This is not the case today.

Some denominations are more progressive than we are on gender equality. The President of the Disciples of Christ is a woman from Oklahoma, Sherry Watkins. A woman is a bishop in the Methodist Church. The ecumenical Officer of President Obama's church is a woman.

Finally, when were you baptized in the Holy Spirit and how has that shaped your life? How has it shaped your views on this particular issue of gender equality?

I was raised in church. Both of my grandfathers left the Baptist Church to become Pentecostal. One of my grandfathers was a son of a Baptist minister. He heard G.F. Taylor preach on the steps of the courthouse in Williamston, North Carolina, and accepted the new doctrine. His family was very upset at his decision to become Pentecostal.

Nevertheless, he joined the Pentecostal church and sought for the baptism in the Holy Spirit for fourteen years before he received the blessing. While I was student at Holmes Bible College, I found his testimony of receiving the Holy Spirit in the church paper, the *Advocate*.

After I was saved and sanctified, I started immediately to seek for the infilling of the Holy Spirit. We would have tarrying services, so I prayed and sought the Lord. I was fifteen or sixteen years old when I was baptized in the Spirit and spoke in tongues. It became an important part of my life and ministry.

The Holy Spirit created a love in my heart for the Word of God, and He became my teacher in the Word. He gave me the strength and the power to live the Christian life and as a young boy to enter the ministry. His anointing makes all the difference in living the Christian life and especially the Christian ministry.

4

OUR SPIRITUAL ETHOS: THE CALL, THE BAPTISM, THE ANOINTING

> *For the spirit that God gave us is no cowardly spirit, but one to inspire power, love, and self-discipline. So never be ashamed of your testimony to our Lord, nor of me imprisoned for his sake, but through the power that comes from God accept your share of suffering for the sake of the gospel. It is he who has brought us salvation and called us to a dedicated life, not for any merit of ours but for his own purpose and of his own grace, granted to us in Christ Jesus from all eternity* (2 Tim. 1.7-9).

Bishop Leggett's interview makes it clear that our rich, spiritual heritage is still alive in the IPHC. The threads of tradition that remain alive can be summed up by a look at three elements which play a major role in the construction of ethos for women preachers:

1. All were called to preach.
2. All were baptized in the Holy Spirit and spoke in tongues.
3. All considered their preaching 'anointed'.

A non-Christian might call this 'charisma', but for the Pentecostal, it is a type of charisma that the Holy Spirit produces through a speaker to call sinners to repentance.

In the end, power must be claimed before truth can be proclaimed, and the stories these preachers had in common lent them the power they needed to gain legitimacy in the IPHC. To put this in a Corderian theoretical framework, generative ethos describes how an autobiographical description of one's call story is an example of how individual ethos calls forth a resonance with a collective ethos because a call story creates the speaker, and it creates her epistemic world shared with her group. As the reader engages with the text, the reader is invited into that world. Speaking is not simply about communicating a message, but about creating identification, understanding, and a shared world. The call to preach is a site of transformation with great dramatic potential in Pentecostal autobiographies for both writer and reader.

The Call to Preach

For early twentieth century Pentecostal preacher Agnes Ozman La-Berge, often cited as the first woman to be baptized in the Holy Spirit with tongues as the initial evidence in the United States, preaching may have been a 'call' extended to every Christian willing to answer it. She says that she was told to study the Bible all the time because 'the days would come when we would be called out to preach and give out the word and have no time to look up a subject'.[1] She may have constructed her 'call' in this way to make the call non-exclusive so that both men and women could answer it. Unlike LaBerge, however, for most Pentecostal preachers the 'call' is an experience where one is singled out by God to preach and is not something everybody has to do or even can do.

The call to preach is openly welcomed by women today, but it was a struggle for early and mid-twentieth century women preachers in the IPHC and in other denominations. The Pentecostal women interviewed by David Roebuck and analyzed by Mary McClintock Fulkerson in her article 'Joyful Speaking for God' almost unanimously professed to a 'struggle to accept God's call'. Harvey Cox labels this as the 'call-refusal motif' that characterizes many early call stories. One of the women interviewed by Roebuck and analyzed by Fulkerson claims that God spoke to her every night until she accepted the call to preach, and another constructs her call paradoxically by outlining how she overcame her own prejudices against women preachers by experiencing the call herself. The folklorist Elaine Lawless asserts that all of the Pentecostal women preachers she interviewed 'resisted the call', with one even claiming that she felt that a fall on the ice, which resulted in her hand being

---

[1] Agnes Ozman LaBerge, *What God Hath Wrought* (repr., New York: Garland, 1985), p. 23.

permanently crippled, was God's way of making her 'pay attention' to her call to preach.

In Scanzoni and Setta's collection of testimonies of women preachers in Evangelical, Holiness, and Pentecostal traditions, they tell us that the Nazarene Mary Cagle claims she felt called but tried to avoid it.[2] When her husband became ill and his life hung in the balance, she tried to bargain with God: she would preach if He would allow her husband to live. She says that God replied, 'Will you do what I want you to do whether I heal your husband or not?' She said that she would; so after her husband's death two months later, she began to preach. Famous Pentecostal preacher Aimee Semple McPherson's call story also tells how she strongly resisted the call to preach until she almost died and felt she had to accept. 'Oh, don't you ever tell me that a woman cannot be called to preach!' she writes.[3]

Like these other women preachers, IPHC preacher Grace Hope Curtis strongly resisted the call to preach but ended with a passionate embrace of it after her daughter's close brush with death. In her autobiography, *Pioneer Woman for Christ*, she tells of praying for her daughter, only a year old, who was very ill.[4] She says she prayed for days and days but finally could do no more than watch her life ebb away. 'We trusted God fully in those days [that is, in faith healing, not doctors]', she writes, 'and we prayed and prayed for her healing, but she continued to lay lifeless for days'. She says that at that point God reminded her of her call to preach, and she tearfully accepted it. She writes, 'As I surrendered I looked down at the baby. She had ceased her death rattle breathing and had fallen into a deep natural sleep'. Later she writes, 'I thank God for the ministry He gave me; although some fifty years ago, it was not as easy as it is today'.[5]

In an interesting parallel to Grace Hope Curtis' dramatic call story, my grandfather Robert Rex, a mid-to-later twentieth-century IPHC evangelist who served most of his career as the Director of

---

[2] Letha Dawson Scanzoni and Susan Setta, 'Women in Evangelical, Holiness, and Pentecostal Traditions', in Rosemary Radford Ruether and Rosemary Skinner Keller (eds.), *Women and Religion in America: 1900-1968* (San Francisco: Harper and Row, 1986), p. 238.

[3] Scanzoni and Setta, 'Women in Evangelical, Holiness, and Pentecostal Traditions', p. 245.

[4] Curtis, *Pioneer Woman for Christ*, p. 16.

[5] Curtis, *Pioneer Woman for Christ*, p. 41.

Evangelism, also validates his position through an emotional appeal based on a sense of social resistance. In his call story, Rex describes walking along a 'narrow wall' in the 'pitch dark'.[6] 'Some kind of power would take hold of me and try to pull me off this wall', he writes, 'then this hand would take hold and pull me back on the wall and guide me for a few more steps'. Finally, upon reaching the other side, he finds Jesus sitting on the throne and, though he can't see Him clearly, he falls down to worship. That's when Jesus asks him to preach.[7] In Rex's case, the dramatic call story might have provided a place for generative ethos to occur for the purpose of winning over his reluctant mother who did not believe in his call to preach, or to validate his administrative positions within the IPHC despite his lack of education (though he acquired this later), or to explain his frequent absences from home to my uncle and mother.

Interestingly, the 'call-refusal motif' does not characterize the transcribed interviews of contemporary IPHC women preachers that I collected in 2004. In fact, the dramatic emotional appeal of these call stories is quite different and resists paradigms that were set by the early to middle twentieth century preachers such as Aimee Semple McPherson and that resonated in the testimonies of ordinary folk such as Curtis and Rex. For example, Charlene West's story begins with a vision one Sunday morning where she saw herself 'going down through Texas and Mexico on through central America to the upper part of South America'.[8] She says, 'From there I saw myself as a small figure on a screen and from there the figure got larger and then disappeared. The Lord spoke to me at that time and he said, "I hold you in the hollow of my hand. I'm going to take you to many nations"'. West says she got the call to preach in a separate encounter.[9]

The late Debbie Whipple of the IPHC's Evangelism USA, who was raised in a Catholic church, says that she received her call to preach as a child. She explains:

> We had to go to mass every day at Catholic school. I remember one day doing that, and I couldn't have been more than ten years old, and of course the priests were always men and they still are

---

[6] Rex, *I Was Compelled by Love*, p. 29.
[7] Rex, *I Was Compelled by Love*, pp. 29-30.
[8] See Charlene West Interview below, p. 81.
[9] See Charlene West Interview below, p. 81.

today, but I remember watching them serve Communion and although I didn't realize it then it was God talking to me and what he said to me was: 'You're going to do that someday.' And not even understanding what was happening, I just looked up at the priest and thought, 'Okay, I'm going to do that someday'. But there's no way I could have done that in the Catholic church.[10]

In contrast, Peggy Eby, who was a leader in the IPHC Women's Ministries for years and who now co-pastors in Houston, Texas, was only fourteen when she was baptized in the Holy Spirit and felt the call to preach.[11] She recalls how she asked God to help her understand what the call meant in a time alone with him:

I talked to God as earnestly as I knew how: 'Lord, show me. What is this feeling of a call about? I don't understand this feeling, and I'm afraid. Also, I'm just a teenager—and a girl!' On the one hand preaching definitely appealed to me. I was not one of those people who reluctantly accepted the call. Because I wanted it so much, I felt I had to question it.

After she prayed, she drew a Scripture card out of a box and it said, 'Before I formed you in the womb I knew you, before you were born I set you apart; I appointed you as a prophet to the nations'. She says that she grabbed her Bible and read the rest:

'Ah, Sovereign Lord', I [the prophet Jeremiah] said, 'I do not know how to speak; I am only a child'. But the Lord said to me, 'Do not say "I am only a child." You must go to everyone I send you to and say whatever I command you. Do not be afraid of them, for I am with you and will rescue you,' declares the Lord. (Jer. 1.6-7)

With that, she says she fell to her knees and said a 'resounding "Yes!"' to God.[12]

---

[10] See Debbie Whipple Interview below, p. 95.
[11] See Peggy Eby Interview below, p. 94.
[12] See Peggy Eby Interview below, p. 92.

The Baptism

The experience of the baptism of the Holy Spirit and the subsequent evidence of speaking in tongues lent the most credibility to a Pentecostal preacher. Learning from each other's stories, not only about the baptism but also how to recognize it and why one would want it, first and second generation Pentecostal preachers knew that to continue preaching for the IPHC meant that they must seek the baptism. While conversion is a change in power from one's self to God, baptism in the Holy Spirit is often spoken of as becoming empowered. If we take Paul as an example, it is a change from either one power (Paul's idea of God as a devout Jew) to a new power (Paul's idea of God as a Jewish-Christian). Or it can be a change from 'self' to God, as Paul imagines it for many Gentiles who convert. Baptism in water is the physical proclamation of conversion for most Christians. However, baptism in the Holy Spirit is a matter of transcending a normal experience of Christianity into an empowered one. The baptism in the Holy Spirit is physical proof of God's approval of the believer and has positive social effects. Cheryl Bridges Johns writes:

> With the inception of modern day Pentecostalism, women, as recipients of the gift of the Holy Spirit, found themselves experiencing a new dimension of freedom. They found themselves preaching, speaking in tongues and giving interpretations, laying hands on the sick for healing. Women became writers, defending their new-found liberty. Many left for the mission field, in spite of the fact that there was little institutional support for their ventures.[13]

The baptism in the Holy Spirit made church ordination irrelevant, Johns argues, although many of the early IPHC women preachers were licensed and/or ordained. For most Pentecostals the 'call' superseded institutional requirements for the right to preach in the early twentieth century, and efforts to put educational requirements on IPHC preachers were not written about until the October

---

[13] Cheryl Bridges Johns, 'Pentecostal Spirituality and the Conscientization of Women', in Harold D. Hunter and Peter D. Hocken (eds.), *All Together in One Place: Theological Papers from the Brighton Conference on World Evangelization* (JPTSup 4; Sheffield: Sheffield Academic Press, 1991), p. 162.

25, 1917, issue of the *Advocate*, almost twenty years after the de-nomination's inception.[14]

In summary, the baptism in the Holy Spirit granted women the authority to preach before the emerging Pentecostal denominations became institutionalized. What's more, the participation of the audience in co-creating this ethos is clear from Edith Blumhofer's claim that 'A person's call—and how others viewed it—was far more important than [ministerial credentials]'.[15] Carol Noren echoes the idea of public recognition as validation when she outlines three areas of authority: traditional, charismatic, and legal rational.[16] In the charismatic type of authority, validation comes through the audience's recognition of that preacher as a leader. The charismatic authority, she says, is the type that clergywomen can most easily ac-cess because traditional authority is limited to males, and legal-rational authority is based upon a person's ability to navigate con-flict that accompanies administrative positions.[17]

Even so, description of the baptism of the Holy Spirit is mini-mized in the autobiographies I analyzed. For example, Grace Hope Curtis never describes speaking in tongues but says she 'shouted all over the church' at one point and then later describes how her sec-ond husband 'became Pentecostal'.[18] Early/middle twentieth cen-tury preacher Lucy Hargis describes her experience as such:

> I received the Holy Spirit baptism July 16, 1922, about midnight and when I came up speaking in tongues, the girls and manager where I worked were all there and they knew then I was one of them that we all had talked about. The religion was so new until the people climbed the seats to see the demonstration of the Holy Spirit and people speaking in tongues.

She says that her husband received his 'Pentecost' later that same year.[19]

---

[14] Johns, 'Pentecostal Spirituality', p. 162.

[15] Quoted in Sheri R. Benvenuti, 'Pentecostal Women in Ministry: Where Do We Go from Here?' *Cyberjournal for Pentecostal-Charismatic Research* 1 (January 1997), <http://www.pctii.org/cyberj/cyberj1/ben.html>.

[16] Carol Marie Noren, *Woman in the Pulpit* (Nashville: Abingdon Press, 1991), pp. 48-49.

[17] Noren, *Woman in the Pulpit*, p. 49.

[18] Curtis, *Pioneer Woman*, pp. 15, 32.

[19] Hargis, unpublished letter, pp. 8-9.

Lennie Rex, my grandmother and the wife of IPHC preacher Robert Rex, wrote that it took her two years of praying before she was sanctified. Not long after that she was baptized in the Holy Spirit at a revival. 'No one had to teach me how to let the Holy Spirit speak in tongues', she wrote. Her mother later told her that 'hundreds gathered [for] they had never saw any one receive the Holy Spirit'. She spoke in tongues for three days until 'just as suddenly as the Lord sent His great power and slayed me under, soaked me through and through with His power, wonderful power, and the Lord spoke to me "Now you can speak"'.[20]

Finally, Wanda Baker, daughter of a Pentecostal preacher, says that two women converted under her mother Ruth Moore's ministry stayed up with her mother all night praying. At the beginning of a sunrise camp meeting service, her mother was 'filled with the Holy Spirit'.[21] The minimal details should not be interpreted as evidence that these experiences were not notable. The baptism was spoken of so much that it falls under the 'it goes without saying' category instead. For Debbie Whipple, it was an experience that came before she really knew what the baptism was supposed to be.[22] Her innocence lends her narrative a truth factor that is unique in relationship to many other narratives.

Also, for these women, the baptism was life-changing, but using it as a tool to gain a position of power was not necessarily the goal so much as it was an unintended benefit of the experience. While it did give early IPHC women the right to preach, for contemporary preachers Charlene West and Peggy Eby, the baptism of the Holy Spirit was linked to their 'anointing' to preach.

The Anointing

The essence of the Pentecostal ethos can be seen in terms of the 'anointing'. The 'anointing' served as validation of 'the call' and of being Spirit-filled. The authority gained by the perception that her

---

[20] Kristen D. Welch, 'Appendix F: Personal Letter, Lennie Cordie Gilcrease Rex, Date Unknown', *Oklahoma Preachers, Pioneers, and Pentecostals: An Analysis of the Elements of Collective and Individual ethos within the Selected Writings of Women Preachers of the International Pentecostal Holiness Church* (PhD Dissertation, University of Arizona, 2007), p. 278.

[21] See Wanda Baker Interview below, p. 115.

[22] See Debbie Whipple Interview below, p. 97.

sermons were anointed gave women preachers the power to profess truths from the pulpit and in their autobiographies; it was an authority we might say is a result of being a charismatic speaker. In her explanation of how the call, the baptism, the anointing, and the urgency of the message in the early twentieth century came together to make a place for 'radical egalitarianism', Estrelda Alexander writes:

> Early Pentecostals held that individuals were empowered through Holy Spirit baptism to do ministry as the Spirit willed. They believed God supernaturally anointed individuals, without regard to social construction, education, or other formal preparation. Proof of one's call lay in the person's own testimony to such a call and in the perceived fruit of a Spirit-empowered ministry, rather than in a formal ecclesiastical system of selection or promotion. Men or women who demonstrated preaching skill and ability to convey a convincing gospel message, and who displayed charismatic ministry gifts and evangelistic ability were urged into action.[23]

Charisma is a term with many connotations and is not an equivocal term for the 'anointing', but an exploration of the term is helpful for understanding the anointing. The Greek term *charisma* comes from the *charis*, which means 'grace' or 'favor'. It is related to the word 'character', which was key to Aristotle's concept of how a speaker constructs credibility or ethos.[24] Charles Barfoot and Gerald Sheppard describe how in the period from 1901 to the 1920s, the time of 'Prophetic Pentecostalism', many relied upon a combination of three elements for a speaker to gain the authority to preach. First of all, the 'call' was the 'only difference between ministers and laity'; secondly, 'the confirmation of the call' was accomplished through the recognition of charisma by the community; and finally the community was characterized by its 'latter rain' beliefs. Barfoot and Sheppard claim that the 'anointing of the Holy Spirit' is the language used to describe charismatic speakers in the early days; then they use Weber's definition of charisma, which focuses more

---

[23] Estrelda Alexander, 'Introduction', *Philip's Daughters: Women in Pentecostal-Charismatic Leadership* (Eugene, OR: Pickwick Publications, 2009), pp. 1-18 (4).

[24] Craig R. Smith, *The Quest for Charisma: Christianity and Persuasion* (Westport, CT: Praeger, 2000), p. 3.

on the group's reception of the speaker than on the speaker herself, to explain how charisma worked.[25]

Certainly audience reception is key to the success of a charismatic speaker, but Craig Smith describes the highest type of charisma as one that can be used to inspire readers or listeners to 'reach beyond the material world and associate in some way with the metaphysical, the transcendent, the spiritual, or some other form of perfection' as the highest level of charismatic ability.[26] While Barfoot and Sheppard seem to suggest that early Pentecostals only gained authority through emerging ideologies, Smith seems to suggest that charismatic speakers may gain authority whether such belief systems are in place or not. Perhaps it is charisma that fuels emerging ideologies and thereby establishes authority.

Nothing is more important than charisma and the anointing when a person wishes to exercise authority from a Pentecostal pulpit. The success of preachers who persuade congregations to partake in the experiences they prescribe is largely due to their charisma in the pulpit, as well as to the work of the Spirit. In Pentecostal circles the charismatic personality was and still is recognized as an authority figure who brings the congregation toward a moral consensus, but today ministers also establish ethos through meeting certain educational requirements required for licensing.[27] The educational requirements, however, do not guarantee a Pentecostal preacher's success. Again, it is the congregation's recognition of the Spirit's anointing of a minister that is essential for success.[28]

Charisma, in coordination with the audience's perception of 'the anointing', is an example of how the preacher's ethos is co-generated to create a sense of the past as well as the sense of the future in a text or speech. Drawing upon biblical precedents from Acts, evidence of the Holy Spirit validates a preacher's right to be in the pulpit and the veracity of what is said while there. While charisma is a secular term, the anointing is a term that stands for the experience of charisma as a result of the involvement of the Holy

---

[25] Charles H. Barfoot, and Gerald T. Sheppard, 'Prophetic vs. Priestly Religion: The Changing Role of Women Clergy in Classical Pentecostal Churches', *Review of Religious Research* 22.1 (September 1980), pp. 4-7.

[26] Smith, *The Quest for Charisma*, pp. 1-2.

[27] Noren, *Woman in the Pulpit*, pp. 48-49. Also, Barfoot and Sheppard, 'Prophetic vs. Priestly Religion', p. 226.

[28] Barfoot and Sheppard, 'Prophetic vs. Priestly Religion', p. 226.

Spirit as a preacher preaches. Ultimately, referring to one's anointing in an autobiographical text, particularly within the shortened space of the interviews I conducted in 2004, reveals a Pentecostal assumption that the Holy Spirit is a catalyst for truth-making in the space of their religious epistemologies and that the anointing is key to what preachers do.

Examples of the anointing that were found in the autobiographies and biographies of Pentecostal preachers illustrate the importance of charisma and the anointing in various contexts. Margaret Muse Oden's description of a service in the early to mid-twentieth century reveals that the location of a service provided special sorts of challenges that could only be overcome by a lively, charismatic speaker. In a one room building, such as a schoolhouse or church, mothers had to nurse their babies and occupy toddlers, fires would have to be stirred, and old gas lights would have to be 'pumped up again' while the preacher 'delivered his soul in the message'.[29]

Evidence of Grace Hope Curtis' anointing and charisma came through stories of her connections to the people. For example, when she writes about preaching in an 'Indian village' near Kaw City, Oklahoma, she says that they were the 'janitor, the musician, the singer and preacher!' 'We would have to turn on the lights, build a fire in the big old wood stove, then in a matter of minutes the house would be full of Indians'.[30] When the meeting was over, she says that 'everyone in the house—little, big, old and young, came up to shake my hand or hug my neck. I don't think there was a dry eye in the building. It makes my tears flow after all these years to think of it'.[31]

In contrast, Wanda Baker describes her mother, early to middle twentieth century Pentecostal preacher Ruth Moore, as 'loved by her people', but not 'flamboyant'. 'She was very shy, very feminine', she says. 'Mother never took on the demeanor of a lot of women that adopted sort of a masculine demeanor. Mother was very shy. She was not a conversationalist. She was a wonderful listener'. To her mother, Baker says her work was a 'calling' that she felt in her heart and 'what she preached, she lived and believed'.[32] Her cha-

---

[29] Oden, *Steps to the Sun*, p. 47.
[30] Curtis, *Pioneer Woman*, p. 26.
[31] Curtis, *Pioneer Woman*, p. 27.
[32] See Wanda Baker Interview below, p. 116.

risma was strong, but not loud or attention-grabbing. Her anointing could reach beyond the quiet exterior to draw in a congregation of listeners.

Charlene West's validation of her charisma and abilities was evident when attendance remained the same once she took over a church in Bakersfield that she had previously co-pastored with her husband before he passed away.[33] Debbie Whipple's charisma was evident in the fact that she never sought out an invitation but was often invited to preach.[34] Peggy Eby's charisma is evident by the leadership positions she's held in Women's Ministries in the IPHC and the invitations she continues to get to speak at 'various women's groups, conferences, and local churches'. She leads Bible studies and does conferences for women called *Women Who Lead* in which she instructs women preachers.[35]

The Call, the Baptism, and the Anointing: Pieces of a Pauline Epistemology

The calling, the baptism of the Holy Spirit, and the anointing were what both distinguished IPHC women preachers as well as what bound them to other Christians and Pentecostal Christians in particular. Without these key three elements, ethos could not be fully built. The bedrock of a Christian epistemology and the model of a Christian preacher's ethos are found in the Pauline epistles, although these letters have been subject to an endless variety of interpretations. The women I studied were all students of Paul's, just as every Christian is, and thus it is not a stretch to claim that ethos is built through their interpretations of Pauline scriptures.[36]

Paul was the master of paradox in the expression of his ethos. He skillfully set up the argument for his ethos as a true Christian minister by describing Christian ministers in 2 Cor. 6.3-7 as 'steadfast' in spite of great difficulties, as 'innocent' in behavior but strong in their 'grasp of truth', as patient and 'kind', through 'gifts of the Holy Spirit', and as gifted with 'unaffected love' and the

---

[33] See Charlene West Interview below, p. 82.
[34] See Debbie Whipple Interview below, p. 99.
[35] See Peggy Eby Interview below, pp. 91.
[36] Paul is especially interesting to me because he was a masterful practitioner of a type of written rhetoric which was often autobiographical.

'power of God'. His self-effacing ethos, built on spiritual purity and strength, highlights unconditional love experienced through the power of God. This ethos is much like the feminine ethos exemplified in the writings of the IPHC women preachers. Elaine Lawless and Mary McClintock Fulkerson remarked on the mother persona of women preachers, and the 'mother in Israel' stereotype in Pentecostal literature evokes a selfless ethos in the hands of a caring shepherd (it is what they called my grandmother when she died). Paul's characterization of this quiet, stoic power is clearly a pattern for women who spent much of their lives reading New Testament Scripture. It is paradoxical because the surface weakness is only a façade for what becomes spiritual power.

Paul also used paradox in his description of the Christian minister, cleverly turning himself into the image of a spiritual warrior as he simultaneously highlighted the humble position of the early Christian:

> We wield weapons of righteousness in right hand and left. Honour and dishonour, praise and blame, are alike our lot: we are the impostors who speak the truth, the unknown men whom all men know; dying we still live on; disciplined by suffering, we are not done to death; in our sorrows we have always cause for joy; poor ourselves, we bring wealth to many; penniless, we own the world (2 Cor. 6.7-10).

Strength framed in weakness is a feminine motif in the construction of ethos, carried through in strands still found in the words of contemporary women preachers.

Ethos, for the Pauline preacher, was built through intimacy with God and humility, not through education, expertise, or rhetorical technique in speaking. The knowledge that was valued is that of God's wisdom, and the preacher's job was to communicate that knowledge to others. The preacher shared 'God's hidden wisdom' as it was 'revealed' through the Spirit because the 'Spirit explores everything, even the depths of God's own nature' (1 Cor. 2.7-10). Therefore, the preacher interpreted 'spiritual truths to those who have the Spirit' and spoke 'of these gifts of God in words taught us not by our human wisdom but by the Spirit' (1 Cor 2.13).

The 'debator', as a representative of those rhetoricians with secular educations, is described as one who is full of worldly knowledge and expertise (1 Cor. 1.20). Similarly, the impetus to put 'worldly' wisdom to the side in favor of spiritual sources of wisdom was a central tenet of early Pentecostalism, but it was throughout the Proverbs scriptures as well. Paul claimed his knowledge and insights came directly from God; it was logical for early-to-middle-twentieth-century Pentecostals to make a similar claim as did the Methodists before them. A literal reading of Scripture led to this new ethos-making and to empowerment that subverted efforts to control who could occupy the pulpit, a position which was formerly limited to only those with an education and who were male.

A literal reading of Scripture also led to a continued mistrust of rhetoric, something even St. Augustine struggled with as a former professor of rhetoric himself. However, it is sophistic rhetoric, not all of rhetorical theory, that is mistrusted by Plato and by many others even in the revival of sophistic rhetoric in the twentieth century. The belief in relativity and the use of rhetoric to communicate probability and not truth remains at the forefront of scholarship today, except the weight of consensus lies on the side of the sophist, not the Neo-Platonist, Christian, or others.

Sophistic rhetoric emphasized human abilities, not spiritual. First Corinthians 2.4 says: 'Christ did not send me to baptize, but to proclaim the gospel; and to do it without recourse to the skills of rhetoric, lest the cross of Christ be robbed of its effect'. 'Conviction', Paul went on to say, comes by 'spiritual power', not 'clever arguments' (2.4). In Paul's epistemology rhetoric was associated with 'mere words', and preaching was accomplished by 'the power of the Holy Spirit' who brought 'strong conviction' (1 Thess. 1.5). However, in 2 Timothy we find Paul instructing Timothy to 'proclaim the message, press it home in season and out of season, use argument, reproof, and appeal, with all the patience that teaching requires' (4.2). Though he did not use the term 'rhetoric', he was explicitly advising that Timothy use rhetorical techniques to argue for the Christian message. Like St. Augustine who came a few centuries later, Paul also returns to rhetoric for its power, but not for its emphasis on relative truth-making or for its emphasis on human pride and intelligence, as was associated with the sophists.

The Analysis: Call Stories

In the first chapter, five elements of ethos were offered as categories for interpreting generative ethos of IPCH women preachers.
Some of these categories can be used to analyze call stories such as
the story of Grace Hope Curtis.

Ethos as the voice of wisdom or authority

The dramatic call story was a way of defending a woman's place in
the pulpit because the co-generation of God-human ethos created
an authority an individual story of an experience might lack. It also
provided evidence that knowledge was not human-generated but a
result of interaction with a living God/the Holy Spirit/Christ. As
an autobiographical story, the call story has verisimilitude that often
goes unquestioned due to empathetic engagement on the part of
the reader. This position creates a place of authority for the writer.
It's her story, and who else can tell it as truly as she can?

Ethos as a bridge to identification with the reader

The similarity of Curtis' story with other call stories also lent veracity to the world she opened for her reader to share, though she did
not mention the other stories. Rhetorical theorist Richard Whately
discusses the weight of corroborative testimonies in the eighteenth-
nineteenth century text, 'Elements of Rhetoric' where he addresses
the use of testimony to refute nonbelievers and to support arguments for 'revealed truth'.[37] Another way these testimonies gain
credibility, as Whately explains, is that the less probable something
is, such as a call story or the baptism of the Holy Spirit, the more it
appears to be true. The reader co-generates ethos through a shared
leap of faith with the writer, accepting what is being said as true
about the person and about what is being said as true about the
God they both know. To accept such truths were a distinct act of
bravery in the early to middle twentieth century; such identification
also carries the thrill of a shared social risk.

The emotional appeal to her reader through her daughter's ill-
ness created levels of identification with readers, and it created a
shared world as described by Corderian generative ethos where the

---

[37] Patricia Bizzell and Bruce Herzberg, (eds.), 'Richard Whately', *The Rhetorical
Tradition: Readings from Classical Times to the Present* (Boston: Bedford/St. Martin's,
1990), pp. 828-30 (829).

reader co-created and thereby validated Curtis' ethos as a 'called' preacher through a process of identification on spiritual and human levels and through resonance with similar call stories in circulation. As noted earlier, generative ethos may be described as commodious and inviting. In this example, the reader is invited to validate Curtis' role, her spiritual relationship with God, and her association with Pentecostalism. Because the reader vicariously lives through Curtis' days of worry, Curtis leads her reader toward her desired conclusion: She had no choice but to accept the calling.

Ethos as a tool for transformation of the reader
If her reader was resistant to a woman as a preacher, Corderian ethos describes how ethos can sometimes act as an element of transformation as the reader's qualities emerge as one progresses through a text and also as the reader works her way through the argument reflectively. Curtis worked to limit the meanings her reader could derive, an idea validated by Corder's theory that addresses elements of how when we choose words we limit our meanings, and hoped to lead her reader to the only acceptable conclusion. Her call story was probably effective in winning many of her resistant readers over to the idea that a woman could be called to preach.

The Analysis: The Baptism and the Anointing

The analysis of how ethos works in the baptism stories helps to explain how the sparse stories are still powerful and could not be left out of a Pentecostal preacher's ethos-making.

Ethos as a tool for transformation of the reader
Against a backdrop of resistance to the key doctrine of linking the baptism of the Holy Spirit with the experience of speaking in tongues, these early writers create an ethos by claiming the veracity of a doctrine and an experience some of them were not eager to embrace. Others use the resistance of outsiders to the baptism of the Holy Spirit to create a position of authority for themselves in the minds of other Pentecostal readers by positioning themselves as a group who knows the truth. After all, how can outsiders know the 'truth' if they can't grasp this central experience? Once a reader has a corresponding experience to draw from, the authority of those who have not experienced the baptism can never be fully rebuilt in

the eyes of those who have. Verification comes through seeking the Holy Spirit baptism; validation comes when the baptism itself happens. The crisis that caused the verification process is resolved, and the reader becomes convinced of the truth of the experience.

Ethos as evidence of charisma
The preacher's 'calling' was verified through her ability to draw an audience toward the core experiences of the IPHC religion. Narratives are used to unify the audience, to teach them the 'language' of the denomination, and to communicate central themes that both establish the speaker's ethos as a member of the Pentecostal faith and appeal to the audience through pathos, drawing upon their emotionally charged religious beliefs.[38]

Ethos as a bridge to identification with the reader
The invention that occurs is active, is physical, is social, is spiritual, and draws upon core themes or narratives. The speaker and the audience synergistically create a new reality that is instantiated in the passing moments. As LeFevre explains, language is not just a 'mirror' of an 'existing reality', but it 'is active in constituting reality'.[39] The ethos generated opens a space for actions that may follow or deviate from the paradigmatic narratives used to communicate an ideology. Yet the new reality is not one that is constructed out of a convergence of human imaginations, but one that is defined in relationship to the very real, very physical, and very spiritual experience described as the baptism of the Holy Spirit.

Conclusion

If we think of community as only our community of the present, we miss understanding what a community truly is. A community consists of those who hold a place of privilege and influence in our religious traditions, like the Apostle Paul, and it consists of family, friends, and neighbors, and it consists of those of like faith. Even the larger Pentecostal community reaches back to William Seymour

---

[38] Some scholars might be interested in this aspect of ethos and wish to research fantasy-theme criticism. 'Fantasy' is a term that can be understood to refer to the interpretation of the real.

[39] Karen Burke LeFevre, *Invention as a Social Act* (Carbondale: Southern Illinois University Press, 1987), p. 119.

at Azusa Street just as much as it does to the couple who started the church in a particular town. So, to speak of a collective ethos is to speak of more than just the people who knew each other in Oklahoma or the grown children who remember them now. It is to speak of the influence of the Paul as well, and it is to speak of the living communion with Christ and God through the Holy Spirit. Our spiritual ethos is an individual stamp on our communities that relates to what has come before as much as to what comes after. For Pentecostals, a reliance on the call story, the baptism in the Holy Spirit, and the anointing in the pulpit are three strands of ethos-making that make our part of the larger Christian ethos our own if one looks closely at the unique, individualized instantiations of the autobiographical evidence left behind.

5

PENTECOSTAL WOMEN PREACHERS OF TODAY

The Lord speaks the word; the women with the good news are a mighty host (Ps. 68.11).

The state of women preachers in Pentecostal denominations is best understood by looking at ways the past has shaped the opportunities and limitations of the present. Pamela Holmes writes that in the past, 'on the surface, at least, it appeared that women performed the same function as men without any interference or objection by the men'; however, this led to the Evangelicals criticizing the Pentecostal movement for allowing women to preach.[1] The reality was that even when women were preaching in Pentecostal movements, they were not allowed to be involved in administrative work. Women were 'accepted but limited, affirmed but restricted', according to Holmes.[2] Estrelda Alexander affirms the fact that the limitation of women is still a problem in many Pentecostal denominations in her introduction to *Philip's Daughters: Women in Pentecostal-Charismatic Leadership.*

Barfoot and Shepphard's oft-cited article describes the progression from acceptance to limitation and restriction in Pentecostal denominations that evolved during the twentieth century; but they claim the cause of the shift is based on exegesis, not on Pentecostals choosing to become less radical. They claim that the period from 1901 to the 1920s can be called 'Prophetic Pentecostalism'; and the period from 1920s to the late 70s may be called 'Priestly

---

[1] Pamela Holmes, 'The "Place" of Women in Pentecostal/Charismatic Ministry since the Azusa Street Revival', in Harold D. Hunter and Cecil M. Robeck, Jr. (eds.), *The Azusa Street Revival and Its Legacy* (Cleveland, TN: Pathway Press, 2006), pp. 297-316 (301).

[2] Holmes, 'The "Place" of Women', p. 302.

Pentecostalism' because the shift is a result of defining preachers as priests instead of prophets, not because churches necessarily became more 'worldly'.[3] Roebuck, however, describes the progression toward restriction as part of the Church of God's rise to the middle-class in 'Pentecostalism at the End of the Twentieth-Century: From Poverty, Promise, and Passion to Prosperity, Power, and Place'. That is, as Pentecostals became more affluent, they began to imitate the rest of society. They became main-stream instead of remaining counter-cultural, and this included the adoption of sexist attitudes.[4]

Carolyn Dirksen's article, 'Let Your Women Keep Silence', describes the progression from acceptance to restriction within the Church of God as well, but she frames it in a different way. She says that while five of the eight founders were women, within just a few years after the denomination was officially formed they lost their power to vote, to hold administrative positions, and to be preachers (a result of a lack of desire).[5] It is a complete reversal of the position taken during the formative years when 'evangelism was the pressing goal of the group, and no boundaries were visible among messengers of the gospel'.[6] Interestingly, her article documented women preachers rejecting more administrative responsibilities, not fighting for them. Dirksen quotes pastor Mary Graves who says: 'I can't get everything done that I'm allowed to do now. I don't think I want to be allowed to do more'.[7] Yet Dirksen's interviewee does point out the difficulties associated with having a male make such decisions for a church, particularly when that male is not a regular member of the congregation, simply to avoid allowing a woman to exercise power.

---

[3] Barfoot and Sheppard, 'Prophetic vs. Priestly Religion', p. 2.

[4] David Roebuck, 'Pentecostalism at the End of the Twentieth Century: From Poverty, Promise, and Passion to Prosperity, Power, and Place', in Corrie E. Norman and Don S. Armentrout (eds.), *Religion in the Contemporary South: Changes, Continuities, and Contexts* (Knoxville: University of Tennessee Press, 2005), pp. 53-74.

[5] Carolyn Dirksen, 'Let Your Women Keep Silence', in Donald N. Bowdle (ed.), *The Promise and the Power* (Cleveland, TN: Pathway Press, 1980), pp. 165-96 (165).

[6] Dirksen, 'Let Your Women Keep Silence', p. 169.

[7] Dirksen, 'Let Your Women Keep Silence', p. 176.

Making a Place

How Pentecostal women made a place for themselves after the early years of the twentieth century required more determination since the denominations were becoming more established and returning to the cultural protocols of the nineteenth century. One argument women used successfully to gain the right to preach was to revive the 'all hands on deck' argument for inclusion. Nineteenth century Methodist preacher Phoebe Palmer used this argument to say that America could not afford for half of the available evangelists to stop working.[8] Compare that to contemporary Pentecostal Rev. Dr. Sheri Benvenuti's observation that 'we are, in a sense, watching the house burn down while wondering which fire truck to use'.[9] The fact that such arguments are still needed proves that they are somewhat ineffective.

In a recent edition of *The Cyber-Journal for Pentecostal-Charismatic Research*, Heather Ackley and Annette McCabe argue that while women of the nineteenth and twentieth centuries have been allowed to earn degrees as pastors and other types of church leaders, they have often been denied positions upon graduation.[10] They say that when evangelicals began to be influenced by dispensational premillenialism they were also being influenced by 'Princeton conservatism and fundamentalism' which drove down the numbers of women preachers. With the increasing influence of the fundamentalist perspective, Ackley and McCabe write, people who had women preachers in their family began to feel ashamed of them, as was described by Donald Dayton in his 1976 book, *Discovering an Evangelical Heritage*. Much of our religious American history has been lost due to this unfounded shame.

The numbers of women being educated at institutions and the numbers working in administrative or faculty positions can help

---

[8] Phoebe Palmer, 'Tongue of Fire on the Daughters of the Lord', in Patricia Bizzell and Bruce Herzberg (eds.), *The Rhetorical Tradition: Readings from Classical Times to the Present* (Boston: Bedford/St. Martin's, 2000), pp. 1100-113 (1108).

[9] Benvenuti, 'Pentecostal Women in Ministry'.

[10] Heather Anne Ackley and Annette McCabe, 'Dynamics of Ministry Training and Ministry Opportunities for Charismatic Women: Socio-historical Perspective of Wesleyan, Pentecostal, and Holiness Women in Ministry in the Nineteenth and Twentieth-Century US', *CyberJournal for Pentecostal-Charismatic Research* 15 (February 2006), <http://www.pctii.org/cyberj/cyberj15/Ackley_McCabe.html>.

provide a more accurate picture of where Pentecostalism is today. In 'Dynamics of Ministry Training and Ministry Opportunities for Charismatic Women', Ackley and McCabe quote statistics from 2001 that state that about 35% of all seminary students at that time were women, and about 31% of all Master of Divinity students were women. About 57% of these women will find paid jobs in the church. The low numbers of women earning these types of degrees is related to having a mostly male faculty. They relate the story of how a woman was hired by Pepperdine University (affiliated with the Church of Christ) only to be introduced by the dean as the 'token woman' on staff. She says that she was told not to form relationships with other women on campus who were interested in women's issues and to discontinue pursuing scholarship concerning women and religion, even though this was the focus of her scholarship to date. Finally, while there are very few women in administrative positions in the IPHC, there are only about 18% in Pentecostal denominations as a whole, which is a much better percentage. Finally, Pamela Holmes writes that despite the growing numbers of Pentecostal women who argue that the idea that women are the equals of men is scripturally sound, many Pentecostal churches still employ patriarchal interpretations.[11]

What follows are three interviews with contemporary IPHC women preachers. Although Debbie Whipple has since passed away, the interviews offer a picture of what the Pentecostal ethos is despite the obvious challenges of sexism still felt today. While it is useful to explain the broader contexts of the lives of these women, it is also remiss to assume those broad strokes represent the whole truth of the life of a woman preacher.

Interview with Charlene West[12]

[We begin with Rev. West's personal testimony.]

I'm the daughter of a minister, of a long line of ministers in fact. I'm the third daughter. My father gave me his name because he despaired of ever having a son. He was Charles H., and I'm

---

[11] Holmes, 'The "Place" of Women', p. 310.

[12] This interview was conducted at Muse Memorial Church, in the summer of 2004. See her autobiography: Charlene H. West, *Life is a Great Adventure: Discovering Truth in the Journey of Faith* (Mustang, OK: Tate Publishing, 2007).

Charlene Helen. So, I think that it must have been prophetic because he gave me his name. I always loved the fact that I was a minister's daughter. I was always super proud of my father, and he was my hero.

I became a Christian when I was very small. I can't remember when I started or learned to pray. But I do remember a definite time in my life when I knew I needed to make a decision for Christ and invite him into my heart. That happened when I was seven years old. And that has stayed active in my life all these years. It's been a long time now.

So, I grew up working in the church, sort of being 'right hand' to my father with things that had to do with his office, such as typing his sermon outlines along with the music and all that. Then I chose to go to Southwestern Pentecostal Holiness Bible College. There I met my future husband. We were married in 1950.

I never aspired to be a preacher. In fact, in one class that I had with the famous teacher R.O. Corvin, he was going through the class asking, 'Who is called to preach? Are you called to preach or not?' When he asked me I said, 'No, I'm not called to preach'. He said, 'Well are you called to be a preacher's wife?' And this brought a lot of laughter, and I said, 'Well okay'. I sort of let it slide. But it was really what I wanted to be. I wanted to be a pastor's wife, and have a family, and live in the pastoral home, and carry on the work that I had seen in my father's life. So, I did. I got married to my one-time sweetheart, the only one I really ever had. That was in 1950.

In 1960 I had a tremendous experience one Sunday morning. I woke up really early in the morning, and my family was still all asleep. It was like there was a dead sleep over everybody, and I was wide awake.

I went over into the den, and that moment I knelt to pray I had a tremendous experience with the Lord. I had a vision, and the Lord really spoke to me. I saw myself—we were living in Ada—but I saw myself going down through Texas and Mexico, on through central America to the upper part of South America. From there I saw myself as a small figure on a screen, and from there the figure got larger and then disappeared.

I didn't understand the vision. I didn't know what it meant. And the Lord spoke to me at that time and he said, 'I hold you in the hollow of my hand. I'm going to take you to many nations'. And, well he never said, 'You're going to preach'. To me, the call to preach would have really been an impressive thing for me.

So, that would have been March of 1960. I struggled on until September of that year when I had a definite encounter with the Lord and he really did tell me that I was to preach. And I said, 'Lord I just ask one thing and that is that you will anoint me with the Holy Spirit when I speak'. And from the first time that I spoke after that I felt a tremendous anointing of the Holy Spirit and everyone in our congregation said yes, she's called to preach. And everybody in the area agreed, because I had already been trained in Bible college and by my father, and it was just like I was projected immediately into the pulpit ministry to help my husband. Also, in the district the pastors there invited me and I just began holding little mini revivals.

A few months later my husband took a trip to the Holy Land and I took charge of the church and the radio program and all of that. So, that was the beginning of my ministry in the pulpit.

At that time I had done just about everything except be a preacher and a missionary. So, this about me going to other nations—I just put that on hold because I thought I'm a mom. I had four children and my youngest, at that time, he was just about four months old. So, I thought this is something for the future and God knows all of that. He will bring it about in his timing.

A few years later, about four years later, I had this urge to learn Spanish. I didn't understand why. One day I was listening to the TV and on channel 13 they gave classes in Spanish. And they were using the same book I used in high school Spanish. I took two years of Spanish at Camino Real. And it just kind of got into my spirit, why don't I go over to OU and see about enrolling over there and pursuing this? I really wasn't thinking about this vision that I had; I just kind of put that on the back burner. I told my husband about it and he said, 'Well if you really want to and can manage your schedule with the family and all'. My youngest son had just started kindergarten.

So, I was able to go to school with the MWF schedule. I was able to leave after my son left for school and get back before he came back. So, it worked out just fine. And the ladies in the neighborhood would take care of him if necessary.

I pursued that until we moved to Bakersfield, California. I had had two years of going to OU at that time. I needed another year to finish, but since it seemed that we were called to Bakersfield that's where I went.

It was there that my husband passed away in 1969. The weekend before he died, he had been in Oklahoma City. And he came back that Friday night and he said, 'You know I heard your general youth director say, if he could, he needed to find someone with some Hispanic studies to chaperone a group of Youth in Action team to Costa Rica'. And he said, 'I volunteered for you'. I said, 'Well what about these four kids?' And he said, 'We'll manage'. We had a lady that was real good; she was like a grandma. So, I said, 'Okay'. This was a Friday night, and the next Tuesday morning my husband died of a sudden heart attack. The Bakersfield church asked me to stay on as pastor. We had just completed two years of a television program. And I did stay on. We stayed on and nothing dropped—attendance did not drop.

Later the youth director called me and said, 'You know I'm still depending on you to take this group to Costa Rica'. And I said, 'Oh, you know the changes that have happened in my life. I don't think that I can do that'. I said, 'I've just been right here with the church'. And he said, 'Why don't you talk to the church board?' And so I did and they said, 'Well you know, Brother West made arrangements for you to make that trip and you've been right here with the church during this time. If you want to go', they said, 'we feel like you should go. We can take care of things here. There are ministers that you can schedule'. It was to be a month. And so I said, 'Well okay'. So that was when I went to Costa Rica. That was in June. I was able to preach in Spanish at that time. I did some preparing before I left so I would be able to. But my Spanish—I could speak better than I was able to understand.

When I got back, the Lord began to bring this vision back to me. And I saw myself going south in the Latin American countries. I saw myself alone, which is something I have never understood. I had never shared this with my husband because I didn't want to be misunderstood. But the Lord brought that all back to me, and it became a real insistence. So finally I decided—after making all kinds of excuses to the Lord, like—'Lord you know they have never sent a widow with kids to the missions field'. A lot of single women had gone, but never a woman with children. 'So', I said, 'I don't think they're going to do that'.

I decided I would just call and talk to the Missions Director, who was Floyd Williams at that time. I thought, 'I'll just put the monkey on their back and if they don't want to send me, then okay'. And you know what he said? 'I've known you for a long time and I believe that if you say you're called, then you are. I'll put the papers in the mail for you right away', and so he did. I got them the next week and it was almost like a book, you know. I filled out all these papers on the doctrine and that sort of thing. And then I had to raise funds. I was still raising funds when I left a year later, the week of my husband's death. I left to come back to Oklahoma to visit my parents and had missionary places and purposes along the way. I went all the way to Florida. I had bought a new Volkswagen van and had driven across the country with all my children, except for Paul the oldest who was in college.

So, that was how I became a missionary. Because I was called. And I've just sort of been almost everything—a teacher, a preacher, an educational director, youth missions, and what-have-you—whatever the need at the particular time. But preaching is a very special part of my life. And there are some people—I mean, they can or they can't. But with me it's a compulsion. I feel that I'm not really happy unless I'm in it. In a situation where I can be sharing the ministry in that way. Preaching is a vital part of my life.

Would you tell me more about your work in South America?

I was in Costa Rica nine years and then I went from there to Venezuela. In that time I became a part of the preaching team and we taught in different parts of Latin America. I was there for thirteen years.

All of the churches there already had a Bible study, but this was to be a notch above that. We taught things like church growth, the gifts of the spirit, and things that maybe weren't emphasized as much in the other subjects. I taught and so did John Parker. We were members of the team teaching together. While I was there, I was sent over to Colombia because we didn't have much over there. While there I began a church.

I came home at the end of '91 in December. I came home because I had felt like I had finished the work I needed to do in Venezuela. I had been there at the very beginning when they didn't have anything there. I had been involved in a number of church planning projects. So, I felt like my time was finished, but I didn't know what the Lord wanted me to do.

I got a map and I put my finger on each Latin country and I didn't feel any drawing toward anything. So, I called the Missions Department and told them that I felt that my time was up here. If they had anything that they needed me to do, I would be glad to consider it. But actually, at this particular time, and all of this is a part of God's time, if a door's not open in an area, well you can't go through it! There was really nothing they could offer me right then. However, at the same time that I was here and talked to them, Bishop Underwood talked to me. He said, 'I just heard today that you are not going to stay in Venezuela'. And I said, 'That's right'. 'What are you going to do?' he asked. And I said, 'Well, I don't know. I just know that I'm through there'. And he said, 'Well, do you have any direct leading?' And I said, 'No'. He said, 'Well, come back to see me tomorrow'.

So, what he did was talk to Brother Leggett, who was the director of Evangelism USA. They needed a director for Hispanic Ministry. We had Hispanic conferences and we had Hispanic churches and people working in different Anglo conferences, but we didn't have anyone working on a general level. So, they had tried to suggest one man and another, but others would say, 'Oh, not him'. Anyway, Brother Leggett had not found anybody that he felt was the right person for it. So, Bishop Underwood told him the fact that I was just home and I might be able to do what he wanted. So, I always felt like part of my success on the mission field was partly due to the fact that I was not displacing anybody. I was willing to go and take something nobody else wanted. For instance, if a church's pastor had left and nobody would take it, they would ask me. I would go and plant a church. I don't think people were ever jealous of me because I was not displacing anybody. I was not a threat to anybody. So, I think that that was one reason that I was able to go into Evangelism USA and become the first director of Intercultural Ministry. And, we were in that for a couple of years and then we broadened the office to become the Office of Intercultural Ministry. I was there for seven years.

The summer before I left, which was in General Conference, I had a very definite experience with the Lord when we were taking communion. And he let me know that my time with Evangelism USA was going to be limited and I would be heading into a different area of ministry. And I didn't know why or what. But it was so strong that I wanted to see Bishop Underwood because I had become a missionary under him and he had become a key person for me to talk to. But he was always surrounded by people. But when I went down to the lobby and he was by himself, I was able to talk to him alone. And he said, 'Well, what does the Lord want you to do?' And I said, 'I don't know'. And he said, 'Well, stay where you are until the Lord leads you otherwise'.

I talked to Bishop Leggett and he told me the same thing. I talked to Dr. Carpenter and he said the same thing. I told him, 'You know I'm leaving this department and you may have someone you would like to put into this position. And if you do, then please feel free to do it'. I said, 'My time is going to be limited here so if you have somebody to put in the position, please feel free to do it'. And he said, 'I don't have anybody. Please stay until you know what the Lord wants you to do'. That was three leaders of the church that all told me the same thing.

So, I didn't leave for any problem or difficulty—at the headquarters or on the missions field. I left because it was God's timing. And I think it's so important to know God's timing. And so I shared this with the department there, and they were all really nice. But Debbie Whipple, she was always really interested in me, would always ask me, 'Has God told you what He wants you to do?' And I would say, 'No'. And finally one day, I just opened my mouth and I said, 'I'd like for us to have a strong Pentecostal Holiness Church here that will train people to branch out into the work and plant other churches and make the church grow, a training center and all that'. After I talked to her, I just went and sat down in my office and started writing. And I wrote all the strategies for our church. I shared it with Dr. Carpenter, and he said, 'We'll support you'. And Evangelism USA supported us for the first year.

We started in October of 1998, and then they supported us for a full year. During that year we were able to get a base of people and we worked on a shoestring. I didn't ever want to take more money. I just always felt like there were other people waiting to start other things. But I always felt like they helped us, and that was wonderful.

We were at one church building for two and a half years but then we went about seven miles southeast over to the Central PH church where my husband and I had once pastored. In fact, we had bought that property for the church. But, they were really nice to us and they said, 'you can come on over and have your Hispanic services here'. So we did. We were there for another two and a half years when the original Muse Memorial church property came open. And it was just like—I knew—it was a tremendous experience of 'knowing' that this was the place God wanted us to be and God just telling me that 'Nothing, nothing, nothing is impossible if you can believe for it. I have the funds for everything you need'.

So, I started writing friends and everyone I knew that had been connected with Southwestern in the past and Bill Anderson, who was the pastor here at the time the church was built. In fact, he spoke during our first service last October, and he has sent money to us a thousand dollars at a time. He helped us raise the hundred thousand dollars we needed for a down payment. As it turned out, we didn't have to raise all of that because our loan had been approved for the $325,000. So, we only had to put up the $75,000 when we signed the papers about two weeks ago. So, we've been through a lot of hurdles.

The church was in terrible condition. The plumbing was awful, and there were leaks everywhere. The carpet was up and out in all the entrances. And all of the pipes under the sinks were corroded. Right away we carried away three big truck loads of junk. It was a challenge. We had people over here working every night except Sunday night for our services. They worked every evening for five months. They were painting, cleaning, repairing, renewing, and rejuvenating. Electric lights, bulbs—everything. And then, when we came in October we had to redo the heating, which only cost us $600 dollars. But there have been a lot of things. We kept the insurance up even though the property wasn't ours. We feel like we're getting it back. But, of course, this week somebody came and banged out one of our doors. But when I told the congregation, we praised the Lord because in everything give thanks and we prayed for the person who did that. And maybe he'll come back here and receive the Lord.

What are some of the things your church has to offer?

All of our services are in Spanish. We are in transition. We want to have a cell-based church. That is, we want to have a church outside of the walls of the church. It's a program that began in Bogota. I was there in February and saw it. Their idea is that the pastor will get twelve leaders and challenge them, and they will reach twelve more to have a hundred and forty four. And so on.

The different cells will have different interests; some for children, for youth. We want the youth to be under the youth leader and to work with twelve, and those twelve will work toward twelve. We have a *pre-encounter* for them to use where they share the four spiritual laws. We also talk to them about deliverance. And then we have an *encounter*. The *encounter* should go from Friday evening to Sunday noon; but we only did the first one that way because our church is not too big, and they noticed the absence of the participants. But a little bit later we will go ahead and have it on through Sunday because in the *encounter* you go through the inner healing and you work toward telling them what the vision is of the twelve and the challenge of multiplying. After the *encounter* we have a *post encounter* for four classes to bring everybody together and help them not to forget what they've learned and not to lose the momentum.

Next, they start in the school of ministry. This is important because in the school of ministry you are teaching them the basics of what they're going to be teaching, and you're telling them how they're going to start their cells. They don't have to be a theologian. When we started this program, we had our ministerial studies sort of like the Bible Institute that we had on the missions field. It covered the whole panorama of the Bible, stuff like theology and homiletics and hermeneutics and those subjects which are very important for the professional minister. But, for the moment, we've sort of put that on the side; we don't want to lose it. But what we're doing right now is we're not training them to be a theologian, we're training them to be a soul winner. Because you know we have our Sunday school and a lot of our people have come into our church through the Sunday school in the past, but that is changing. There are a lot of Sunday schools that are giving information, but not teaching people to be soul winners. So, our endeavor is to train soul winners.

A lot of people have said, 'I don't know what to teach if I'm going to teach in a Bible cell'. There are different ways of doing it, but some will have a copy of the pastor's outline for the sermon, for instance. I've thought about giving them a fill-in-the blank outline, and then they fill in the blanks. Then in the cell they go over questions like 'What was it that impressed you?' or 'Did the Lord show you something else that wasn't said in this scripture?'

So, you have the whole gamut. What those people want to do is bring in the unsaved, people who don't have churches. We want to bring in people, invite them into our homes because a lot of people will go into a home that won't go into a church. So, whenever they go to a Bible study cell, you start giving them the four classes beginning with the *pre-encounter* so that they can become a cell leader too. That takes a process of several months and gives them time to mature as Christians.

So this began in Bogota. I was there in February, and this vision of the twelve has absolutely gone around the world. It is not a denomination. They believe in Holiness. And they believe in the Baptism of the Holy Spirit. And, they really, really emphasize the cross and getting rid of anything in your life that isn't like Christ. I saw people from our church and people I knew from Hawaii. I saw the superintendent of the Filipino work here and the superintendent of the work in Spain. There were people there from all of the continents. It was a joy to me to see them because I knew these people. They didn't know each other, so I got to introduce them. Of course, when I got there, I also met with the superintendent of the Venezuela people, one of my spiritual sons, and so I got to be with a lot of people that I had seen grow up in the church in Venezuela. So, that's where my church is at right now.

Sunday night we probably had a hundred and twenty-five in the service. We are running around a hundred. We've lost a few people. We've seen the enemy fight to try to disrupt people over little things. So, I've really had to warn the people that the enemy doesn't want us to do this, that this church is invading his territory.

There's a lot to be done, and the Lord has put us here to do it. I've warned people that we are here in a spiritual battle. On Tuesday through Friday morning from five until eight we're open for prayer, so I'm here at that time. And on Tuesday night we're having classes to teach people to speak English. And then Wednesday night we're having our *post encounter* right now. They need to do that in order to go into the school of leaders. That meets on Saturday evenings. Friday nights our children meet here. We have a children's praise group that have little white outfits and banners.

You have a thriving ministry and seem to be very busy!

When I was working for headquarters, you know, I traveled a lot with the department. They asked me to direct the district in the Minnesota area; so I would go up there three times a year, and I did other things, seminars and studies. But, usually, I was in Oklahoma City, and when the day was over I could come home. I could work out in the yard and stuff, but this, this is in the day, it's in the evenings, and it's in the nights. Brother Leggett called me 'Mrs. Caleb' because I was at my age starting this venture. But the Lord doesn't call you to do something without giving you the strength to do it. So, I had a wonderful time of prayer recently with my daughter. She has been a missionary in Venezuela for fifteen years. They came to Venezuela before I left. They came; and when I left, they stayed on. And then they planted a church, and then they were in Spain for fifteen months. Now they're waiting to go back to Spain. Leaving a legacy is important.

What else have you been doing?

Well, I was working on my doctorate, too, but I had to put it to the side for a while. They had quite a bit of revisions they wanted me to do on my dissertation, even going back to my title. But I'm paying $1700 a year for being in this program and in the last couple of years I've really questioned if I was supposed to be doing that.

Interview with Peggy Eby[13]

When did you become a member of the International Pentecostal Holiness Church?

I was about 9 years old when my parents became followers of Jesus. We had moved to Sapulpa, OK, and the pastor of the local Pentecostal Holiness Church visited our home. He came back regu-

---

[13] This interview was conducted in Tulsa, Oklahoma, on July 24, 2004. Rev. Eby had traveled to Tulsa from Houston to preach at Evangelistic Temple on the following Sunday.

larly until my dad agreed to visit. On that first visit, Dad and Mom decided that we should be a church-going family, and that was the church we joined. I've been a part of IPHC since that day in 1954.

When did you become a Christian?

I cannot remember a time when I did not have a 'heart for God'. But just before my seventh birthday, my cousin attended a Vacation Bible School. While we were playing one afternoon, she told me, 'I got saved today'. I asked her to explain 'getting saved' and her response was, 'That's when you ask Jesus to live in your heart so you can go to heaven when you die'. Of course, I wanted to 'get saved' too. We climbed into the back seat of my parents' car (a 1949 black Chevrolet), and I knelt in the floor and asked Jesus to come into my heart. It was a profound experience that I have never forgotten and have held on to securely. I wasn't perfect, by any means, but there was never a time when I did not want to follow Jesus.

During the next few years I had only occasional visits to church with grandparents and friends but no regular church attendance. Even though I had no real example of prayer in my life, I earnestly prayed and interceded for my parents to come to know the Lord.

Do you have a regular church that you pastor?

No, not at this time. We have pastored churches in the past, but presently we are working in cross-cultural missions. My husband and I have an organization called Mission Catalyst International, which is an interdenominational missions program aimed at training nationals to plant churches among the least-reached people groups in the world. Jim, my husband, does this work full time, and I travel with him two or three times a year. I do conferences for women called *Women Who Lead*. It is exciting to see women around the world who are serious about taking the Gospel to every nation.

I also speak by invitation here in the United States in various women's groups, conferences, and local churches. At the present time I lead a couple of weekly Bible studies for local churches in the Houston area, and I have a small group of ladies that I disciple on a weekly basis. We are walking through the whole process of what it really means to be a follower of Jesus. I also serve on the General Women's Ministries Board (IPHC), which gives me an opportunity to do a number of things related to Women's Ministries such as retreats and conferences.

How do you receive so many invitations to preach?

Because I have been in the International Pentecostal Holiness Church for many years and my husband has been a denominational leader, I've had many doors open to me. Also my work on the Women's Ministries board has kept me visible to women's groups across the nation.

When did you first feel the call to be a preacher?

I was fourteen. My desire was to be totally given to God for His will and purposes for my life. I was passionate for witnessing to people and for the work of the Lord—whatever that was. In that era in my personal life and church life, there seemed to be only three avenues for people who were 'on fire for God'—to be a pastor, an evangelist, or a missionary. So I had told God, in prayer, that I was willing to do anything He asked of me.

One day, during this period of struggle with this sense of call and not understanding what it was, I came in from school to find Mom out with my little sister. Since I had the time alone I knelt down in the living room and began to pray. I talked to God as earnestly as I knew how: 'Lord, show me. What is this feeling of a call all about? I don't understand this feeling, and I'm afraid. Also, I'm just a teenager—and a girl!' On the one hand preaching definitely appealed to me. I was not one of those people who reluctantly accepted the call. Because I wanted it so much, I thought I had to question it.

After my prayer, I stood up and put my school things away. When I walked through the house, I saw a small box with tiny cards which had Scripture verses on one side and a thought for the day on the other. I randomly pulled one out and there was my answer: Jeremiah 1.5, 'Before I formed you in the womb I knew you, before you were born I set you apart; I appointed you as a prophet to the nations'. I grabbed my Bible and read the next few verses: '"Ah, Sovereign Lord,"' I said, '"I do not know how to speak; I am only a child."' But the Lord said to me, '"Do not say 'I am only a child'. You must go to everyone I send you to and say whatever I command you. Do not be afraid of them, for I am with you and will rescue you," declares the Lord' (Jeremiah 1.6-7). With that command and promise I fell on my knees and said a resounding 'Yes!' to God.

I began receiving invitations to speak in youth meetings in various churches. From that point on I preached almost every weekend. During the summers I preached in revivals and church camps. I preached in jails, open-air meetings—sharing God's word with others was the delight of my life.

I started talking about my own life and how God always has a plan no matter what our 'resume' might be. I ended by saying that I felt that I had wasted some of my life when I wasn't a Christian.

With God, it is not a matter of wasted time because He never wastes anything, even our mistakes. Even the years that we call 'wasted', God will use them to weave into the fabric of who we are and the message we have to give. It may appear to you that you wasted those years, but God sees them from a totally different perspective. Perhaps they were wayward years, but God was weaving them into the total fabric of who you are and more than likely is using them to give you a passion for and an understanding of this generation who question everything and resist everything that is traditional—so it is certainly not a waste.

How many children do you have and how has being a mother affected your ministry?

I have three children, a daughter and two sons. When Jim and I married we immediately started to Bible College. During my second year I became pregnant with our first child, and my college career came to a halt. We were pastoring a small church at the time, and I preached regularly in the Sunday evening services. Two more children were born, which brought about huge changes in my life and ministry.

Following that pastorate, my husband became director of Lifeliners International, the denominational youth ministry. This job required extensive traveling and because the children were small I did very little public ministry. My 'ministry' revolved around three young children who needed my constant attention. This was a very important time in my life, but also a difficult time. I was accustomed to being 'up front' in ministry, but now my husband was the 'up front' person. He traveled all over the world, and all I got was a suitcase full of dirty clothes. Let's just say that this was character-building time for me.

I had a remarkable experience with God one day when I was sort of moaning about my lot in life. I said, 'Lord, why did you call me to preach? I'm doing nothing but changing dirty diapers and wiping runny noses'. I felt His response in my spirit: 'If you do nothing else in life, give Me three disciples that are totally committed to me and your life will not be in vain'. At that point I laid down my driving desire to be an evangelist and saw the value of raising my children to know God and to serve Him.

Have you felt any challenges because you are a woman?

At the beginning of my ministry I felt no resistance from the leadership of the Pentecostal Holiness Church. However, I do remember one revival when a delegate from another denomination came over to visit with me in order to correct me on my theology because he thought I was not a legitimate minister (because I was a woman). I was unable to respond with sufficient theological understanding, and saying that I 'felt called' wasn't enough for him.

Pentecostal churches were very open to my ministry. It appears that having a woman preach or teach does not present a problem, but when it comes to having a place of leadership, there is definitely a 'stained-glass ceiling'. Personally, I am not an administrative leader (I am quite happy with preaching), but many women who are called to preach are highly qualified as leaders.

The IPHC has licensed and ordained women for many, many years. However, relatively few women have become pastors or church planters. There have been a number of single women who were missionaries, but that number has significantly declined in recent years.

Tiny steps have been taken to open more doors for women, but much remains to be done. The church will miss some valuable leadership qualities if women are not welcomed into that arena. I believe every church board should have qualified women serving alongside the men.

If lasting change is to happen, church leadership must become intentional about including women. This denomination (IPHC) as well as others, has women who are wise, intelligent, spiritual, and who have strong leadership gifts. Many women (who are preachers) co-pastor with their husbands. They choose not to simply be the pastor's wife. They share teaching, preaching, and administrative responsibilities.

When the Bible talks about the creation of mankind in His own image, it says 'male and female created he them'. It takes men and women together to express the image of God to the church and to the world. I believe that church leadership will be lacking a powerful expression of God's character if women are excluded.

When did you become baptized in the Holy Spirit?
I was fourteen. It was during the time of understanding my 'call' from God and my desire to know Him in a deeper way.

Have you experienced any challenges? Has the Pentecostal religion restricted you?
The local church I grew up in was very legalistic. There were lots of rules that applied primarily to women—no makeup, no jewelry, no short hair, no short sleeves, no slacks, etc. It took me many years to deal with all those restrictions.

More recently, a challenge I have faced with church leadership is a feeling of being patronized but not valued as a woman.

I do not believe being Pentecostal has restricted me. Since the 1960s and the charismatic renewal, Pentecostalism is more mainstream. Pentecostals are the largest group of evangelicals around the world.

Interview with Debbie Whipple[14]

When did you become a Christian, get called to preach?
I'm originally from Kansas City. I came to Oklahoma in my early 30s. I was born and raised there. I'm from an Italian Catholic background. I got really and truly saved when I was twenty-five years old. Up until that time I was in a Catholic church and went to Catholic schools. As far as the call—it was probably after I had my two children that I really—I was divorced at the time—and I really

---

[14] This interview was conducted in Debbie Whipple's home in Oklahoma City, Oklahoma, on July 17, 2004.

sensed the Lord leading me to go to school—to go to Bible college. I didn't really know I was called to preach *per se*, but looking back I think I've been called since I was a young child because I did strange things that kids don't normally do. I remember, just in the middle of the day, I would always go into church, the Catholic church, all by myself—and I couldn't have been more than eight or nine years old—and go up to the front of the church to the altar, and I would kneel down and pray and talk to God. Looking back, that's strange. Not a lot of kids do that. But that was just normal to me. I just wanted to do that. I just liked being there.

There were three or four specific things I would pray for all the time. We had to go to mass every day at Catholic school. I remember one day doing that, and I couldn't have been more than ten years old, and of course the priests were always men and they still are today, but I remember watching them serve Communion and although I didn't realized it then it was God talking to me and what he said to me was: 'You're going to do that someday'. And not even understanding what was happening, I just looked up at the priest and I thought, 'Okay I'm going to do that someday'. But there's no way I could have done that in the Catholic church. I think now lay people do serve communion, but you're talking about thirty-seven years ago, and I felt like that's what I was being told in my spirit. So looking back, I think now that was all very strange.

I was in the Catholic church until I was twenty-five years old, but in the Catholic church back then I couldn't take communion any more if you were divorced. That was a very hard, hard thing for me because I had such experiences with God as a young child. I made my first communion, and that's a big deal in the Catholic church. I remember like weeks before my first communion I had a dream. I was kind of flying and there was a Eucharist, we called it 'hosts' back then, and in this dream I was flying around and I was picking all these wafers off this tree. So getting ready to make my first holy communion was a big deal, and so I was all into that.

Then the day I made it, we always made a big to-do about that kind of stuff in the Catholic church, and my family had a big party. Whenever anybody made their first holy communion, we had a big party. So it was my party and my day.

So, I remember playing around in the backyard telling my older cousins that I feel something inside; I feel so different inside. They looked at me like I was crazy. And that was it.

And so looking back on all these little things, I was having a walk with God that I didn't even know I was having. Now when I probably had my first truly repentive experience, I was again in the Catholic church; it was on a Good Friday. They would have the stations of the cross. The stations of the cross are the twelve stations or stops Christ made from the time he went before Pilate to the time he was crucified. And what would happen is that the priest would walk you through the stations, and on the wall they have icons at each station. You walk and he explains what's going on.

When we got to the station where he fell under the weight of the cross, where Simon had to help him pick it up, I remember feeling the weight of my sin and I remember falling down crying and the nuns just walked on around me. They don't lead you in a salvation experience in the Catholic church. There's never a real born again experience. You know Christ died for your sins. You know Jesus took away the sins of the world. You know all this stuff. But you don't ever really make that confession. You make it in every mass service you make it, you say the Catholic creed, you say Christ died for my sins to take away the sins of the world.[15]

I remember crying and crying and feeling the weight of my sin and actually saying, 'I'm sorry, I'm sorry'. The nuns and other people just walked around me and went on with the rest of the stations, and I composed myself and went on. Now I look back I realized that was my first truly repentive experience with the Lord.

I went on with my life and got married the first time in the Catholic church. We divorced, and I had my time away from God. It was a really sinful time in my life. I didn't know a thing about Pentecost. I never set foot in another church. I was raised that you never went to another church. It was almost a sin to step foot outside a Catholic church. One time I went with a Methodist friend of mine, but outside of that I had never set foot in another church. Didn't know anything about it.

---

[15] Readers should allow for the idiosyncratic experience of religion and should not take Rev. Whipple's experience of Catholicism as a definitive statement of theology or practice. It is simply a description of her experiences in that church.

So I was living in a house in Kansas City, and we had divorced and I realized what a sinner I was and had been for the last three or four years. And I began telling God that I was sorry, I was sorry, please forgive me. And the next thing I knew, I fell—bam!—fell flat. I remember thinking that I didn't feel myself hitting the floor. And I was babbling something. Didn't know what on earth—My mind was telling me that God was casting me down because I was such a sinner—so I got up and went on with my way.

I had a cousin who had married a girl who was Assembly of God, and he and I were really close. And they came over one day, and I told them what had happened. And he said, 'I want you to come to church with me'. And from that day I went, and that was the beginning of my salvation experience.

So, what I find really different about my life is that all of that happened to me when I didn't know anything about it. I never saw anybody—I didn't even know people were slain in the spirit. I didn't know what it was, and it happened and I remember that it didn't hurt. I remember, all this stuff went through my mind—I fell, and it didn't hurt. And I was babbling something, so I assume I got the baptism and was filled with the Spirit all at the same time. So, everything kind of fell in place after that. That was my initial experience. I was twenty-five. Then I got remarried, had my two kids, then I got divorced again.

It was to be my second divorce. Then I moved to Oklahoma. My brothers moved here, my parents moved here, I moved here, my husband left me here. He was a non-Christian.

So, that's when God really, really called me to preach. Well, actually the calling was: 'Study to prove thyself worthy'. I was reading my Bible, and that was the calling. So, I didn't really know what I was doing. In school, when I was in junior high, looking back again I was very ... I was the nerd of the school, didn't have a lot of friends and no dates and all that business. But in speech class, for some reason—and again, it was the calling—I delivered a speech. In the whole time I was there, I delivered one speech. And, it was such a moving speech that I ended up doing it for the whole school, and they tape-recorded it.

So you knew you had a gift?

I didn't even know it really. I knew I enjoyed it. And the techniques I learned in speech class I still use in my sermons today. And they make it very easy for me. For some reason, that class just stuck. It was easy; I understood it; I enjoyed researching it. I enjoyed putting it all together, and I still use that method today. I try to get away from it and do something different, and I just can't. So that calling was always there. I didn't always know what was happening.

So, then I went to Southwestern. When I got out of college, I got my license. And after that I got ordained.

Where did you preach?

All over. Yesterday I preached at Church of the Servant, the United Methodist Church. I did their women's Bible study. There is no rhyme or reason to it. I've been to the Semor-Johnson Air Force base, the Family Air Force retreat, I do women's retreats, I speak in churches—

It doesn't matter the denomination?

Apparently not (laughter). I just go wherever the door opens.

I work in evangelism, and I do prayer walks. I am the Prayer Walk Coordinator for Evangelism USA. Which, I go to the church plants, and I do a Prayer Walk for them. It is an all day Saturday thing with a Friday night service. I am the World Intercession Network Conference Director for the Home Missions Conference. So, there's really no rhyme or reason to what I do. I've been asked to speak in Guyana, South America, and that's the first time I've been asked to speak out of the country. That is October 11th through the 19th.

Do these invitations just come, or do you seek them out?

I never seek out an invitation.

What sets a PH preacher apart is that his/her sermons come from the heart. What do you do to prepare? What do you do first when you get an invitation?

First, I say, 'Oh God, what do you want me to say?' (laughs) I notice that I have gone from 'What am I going to do?' to 'Show me what you want, and I'm going to trust that you're going to give it to me'. So it has been a turn of faith for me. From that little ritual—

'What am I going to do?' to 'Okay, what do you want me to say?'—I know there's something, and 'I'm just going to believe that you're going to give it to me'.

And I pretty much don't start with paper and pen until I get something, and then I might jot it down. And I'll have notes everywhere; because I have an eight to five job, I can't give total focus to that message. So it's in the car, doing the dishes, fixing the bed, at night, first thing in the morning, at work I'll jot something down that is in my head. And after a few days, I kind of get an outline and pray and talk to God, and I pretty much have to have an ongoing conversation with God all the time. So, that's how it all comes together, and then I do manuscripts. I'm a manuscript kind of preacher. I'll write out every word, every joke, every emotion; and I take the yellow highlighter, and I go down the manuscript and I highlight all of the important things that need to come out. I've tried to go back and do an outline, but I'm just not comfortable because for me the anointing comes in the preparation. As I prepare, I really sense the spirit of God and the anointing of God. And so I'm writing down every word that I hear him say. And then I pretty much memorize it, go with the flow and preach it. I definitely listen to the voice. If he says something while I'm talking about it, then I say it.

Do you use stock sermons, or are all of them inspired and original?

I do not, but I definitely see the benefit in that for a preacher who has to preach several times a week. However, I do use some things that God has shown me over and over. For example, as my kids have been leaving the home, it has been very, very difficult; and they have been drawn to my other family members—my brothers and sisters and their families. They live different lifestyles than we live, have more money than we have, and when I was talking to my mom on the phone about them she said, 'Now we shouldn't be jealous over the stuff other people have'. And when I hung up, I thought, 'I'm not jealous of the stuff that they have. I'm jealous of the influence that they are having over my children'. And just like a light bulb, I realized: that's what the jealousy of God is. I never understood it when I read that God is a jealous God. What do I have that God could be jealous of? He's not jealous of anything that we have—he's jealous of the influence those things have over us. So, if they have more influence over us than he does, that's what he's jealous of. Just like I was jealous of the influence other people were having over my children, that's how God is with his children. Whenever we let something influence us more than him—if I think, if I act a certain way, what is so-and-so going to say about it? And that's more important to him—that's what he's jealous of.

How do you fit into the history of the IPHC?

I went to Southwestern because that's where God led me. It could have been anything under the sun, and it wouldn't have mattered because God called me. I was saved in an Assembly of God church. I went to the Bible college. I remember at the time that the PH college did not license or ordain divorced people. But I can remember walking on the college thinking—'Lord, I know you called me; and if I never have a credential, I know I'm a minister'. Through circumstances I was drawn to the church and Muse memorial, and then I got the job; and as soon as I went, it was at that General Conference that they decided that if you were divorced you could be ordained.

So, I say that to say that I didn't care where I was because I knew that God had led me there. I mean, I know little bits and pieces (they started in Falcon), but it didn't matter. It was where God said to go—which likewise when things come up that are not scriptural, then it helps me not to run off. I don't leave because I don't agree with something that somebody said.

Are there any kinds of challenges that you have faced because you're a woman preacher?

There was a time when my husband used to tell me, 'Stay at your job because God is going to open up something there'. And I remember I was on the steps to the Bishop's office and I thought, 'No, nothing's going to happen to me because the men won't let it happen to me. And just when I got to the top step, God asked me: 'Am I not bigger than the men in this building?' And I had to stop. My answer was not immediate because I didn't know. I knew he was bigger. I didn't know if he would do it. I knew he had enough power to do it, but I didn't know. Then I thought, 'Of course, you're bigger'. So, at that point things changed and doors started to open. So, I really haven't had obstacles in that way.

I've learned that when you keep your place and be still that God opens doors; and when he does, usually I have men pushing me forward, pushing me to get out there. I just had an elder in my old church come up to me and tell me that you really need to get your ministry solidified; you really need to get your non-profit status. And it was like when he told me, I was hearing God tell me, 'It's time. Do it'. So, I've found that men are opening doors for me. I don't ever have to open a door for myself. Things may not move as quickly in my life as far as ministry goes, but I feel like the things I am doing have a lot of impact.

I don't have a lot of steps, but I have huge steps. I was the first secretary woman to be asked to speak at a conference two years ago. And about two weeks before I was asked to speak, the Lord told me to get my notes in really good order; and I did. About two weeks later my boss asked me to be a speaker, and I said, 'I did' because God told me to do it. So it was ready.

So I may go six months without a speaking engagement, but then there may be something really significant in the kingdom of God kind of thing. So, I'm not in a normal church preaching every week. That's not the route God has called me to. Now, that's the normal route you think you're supposed to go.

Do you see the fruit of your ministry?

They're so geographically spread out. I don't see it, but I hear about it. I'll get word back. I know it's fruitful. I don't ever doubt about having an impact. I see it on the spot, also.

Do you mentor any women that want to be preachers?

I have several people that I mentor at some level, but not anyone that wants to be a preacher. I have people that mentor me. That's the level I'm at.

6

CONCLUSION

We are God's handiwork, created in Christ Jesus for the life of good deeds which God designed for us (Eph. 2.10).

Understanding the various contexts that affect the way we interpret an autobiographical text is vital for understanding how ethos is generated. Theresa Enos writes:

> Effective ethical argument arises from the union of speaker and listener, writer and reader; the opening up of a world holding within it values that both participants adhere to underlies the whole concept of ethos. Only through ethos can the participants in a discourse achieve identification.[1]

Emerging Ethos of the IPHC

Opening up the 'world' of the IPHC's history and theology by no means opens inquiry into a static entity. The IPHC continues to develop in praxis, and though they may be defined as being conservative in many ways, the denomination's leaders are not 'so bound by dogma, arrogance, and ignorance' that they cannot 'see a new artifact, hear a new opinion, or enter a new experience,' if we may use Jim Corder's terms used to describe the way histories, even self-histories, are always in the process of being made and remade.[2] Even though the texts I analyze are written, as Enos argues, 'the

---

[1] Theresa Enos, '"An Eternal Golden Braid": Rhetor as Audience, Audience as Rhetor', in Gesa Kirsch and Duane H. Roen (eds.), *A Sense of Audience in Written Communication* (Newbury Park, CA: Sage, 1990), pp. 99-114 (101).

[2] Jim Corder, 'Argument as Emergence, Rhetoric as Love', *Rhetoric Review* 4.1 (September 1985), pp. 16-32 (17).

text has a presence', and its presence cannot be ignored.[3] The auto-biographies written by IPHC members create truth, and their 'rhetoric becomes a way of knowing'. The texts are epistemic rhetoric; the writers create their sense of individual and collective, denominational selves through the texts they write. These individual and collective selves draw from larger and localized historical and theological contexts that are developed and redeveloped over time.

The direction of the church will be a process of developing a new ethos, both individual and collective, both material and spiritual. It is a product of discourses, of written language, but more than that, of hope. As this book illustrates, we have a troubled history. Less than a hundred years after the death of Queen Elizabeth, Mary Dyer was hanged on June 1st, 1660, in the Boston Commons. Her crime? Witnessing in public to the Puritans.[4] Women preachers, prophets, exhorters—call it what you will—were not welcomed in the New England colonies in the seventeenth century and would not be welcomed or supported by most of those adhering to any version of Protestant faith until the twentieth century, when roughly ten percent of the American Christian population on the whole would find the idea of women's equality acceptable.[5] In fact, it would not be until four hundred years later that first and second wave feminist protests would finally push Americans into change. Though the battles are still characterized as ugly, bitter, and divisive, both Christian and non-Christian women would emerge in much greater numbers as leaders, as speakers, as politicians, as doctors, as professors—as whoever they wished to be—after these battles were waged successively in public arenas, in corporate arenas, in private homes, and even in churches.

Yet the tinges of bitterness between Christian women and feminists remain. Christian women do not identify themselves with the vernacular definition of feminism because it has so often been reduced to signifying those ultra-liberal, secular feminists who have publicly and loudly denounced Christ, denounced unity with men,

---

[3] Enos, "'An Eternal Golden Braid'", p. 102.

[4] Catherine A. Brekus, *Strangers and Pilgrims: Female Preaching in America, 1740-1845* (Chapel Hill: University of North Carolina Press, 1998), p. 30; 'Quaker Mary Dyer', <http://www.mass.gov>.

[5] 'Christians for Biblical Equality' (2010), <http://www.cbeinternational.org>.

and denounced valuing the family in the most extreme iterations of what they mean by 'freedom' and 'equality'. As J. Lee Grady argues in *Twenty-Five Tough Questions About Women and the Church*,

> Modern feminism is not really feminism at all, since true feminism is the belief that women have God-given rights and human dignity. Many modern feminists have abandoned any mention of faith, and some have, in fact, embraced New Age Spirituality and goddess worship.[6]

Grady points out that historically, first-wave feminists were Christians who pushed social issues, such as the right to vote, in order to empower women.[7] 'The early pioneers of women's rights', he goes on to say, 'who most certainly opposed abortion and homosexuality—would have been horrified if they could see that feminism has degenerated into a pagan philosophy'.[8] Unfortunately, the reduction of the definition of feminism to these extremist views allows men and women to use the term as an accusation, and accusing women of being 'feminist' destroys their careers in the church. Thus, the tension over what gender equality is and what it means in a Christian epistemology is still much debated. Another central question I have explored in my studies is how women have remained submitted to Christ and united to husband and family while still embracing social and spiritual equality. And, of course, the question of how women have successfully justified their place in the pulpit was key to my exploration of the autobiographical texts I collected.

Even though the International Pentecostal Holiness Church does not exclude women as preachers, the inclusion of women as administrative leaders has met with little support. In 1996, the IPHC held a 'Solemn Assembly' and repented of several sins, one of which was male domination.[9] Like so many who have argued for a woman's right to be treated as equal, they used Gal. 3.28 to explain their stance, writing, 'The apostle Paul declares that "there is

---

[6] J. Lee Grady, *Twenty-Five Tough Questions About Women and the Church* (Lake Mary, FL: Charisma House, 2003), p. 163. See also Rosemary Radford Reuther, *Sexism and God-Talk: Toward a Feminist Theology* (Boston: Beacon Press, 1983), to see an example of Grady's claims about feminism.

[7] Grady, *Twenty-Five Tough Questions*, p. 162.

[8] Grady, *Twenty-Five Tough Questions*, p. 163.

[9] Shirley Spencer, 'Solemn Assembly Marks New Beginning for IPHC', *International Pentecostal Holiness Advocate* 80.4 (November 1996), pp. 4-13.

neither Jew nor Greek, slave nor free, male nor female (their emphasis), for [they] are all one in Christ Jesus'".[10] They go on to say in the 'confession': 'We, the men of the Pentecostal Holiness Church, confess that we have not honored the precedent set forth in God's Word. Often, we have not treated our wives as equal partners in marriage and ministry.... We recognize the sin of male domination and acknowledge that we have withheld from women places of honor in the church. We have not affirmed the ministries of qualified women by releasing them to serve in places of leadership. We also have shown inequity regarding their wages'. It is a sign of hope that the Solemn Assembly has not been forgotten. It appears on the current IPHC website and is clearly central to their history and identity as a Christian organization.

However, at the time of writing my dissertation in 2006, a full decade since the Solemn Assembly, I guessed that it was fair to assume that practices toward electing or hiring women to hold leadership positions at the IPHC Headquarters should have changed. I was wrong. The IPHC's official website in 2006 showed few women served in leadership positions within the different ministry departments. I found an all-male board for the Church Education Ministries Department, a male chairman for the Chaplains' Ministries, and an all-male assortment of directors in Evangelism USA. While I expected to find that the leadership of Women's Ministries was female and I knew the Bishop was male (a position always held by a male), World Missions was perhaps most revealing in terms of the gender divide. It listed eleven regional ministries coordinators, all of whom are male, four overseas ministry coordinators, all of whom are male, and three of the four directors, including the Executive director, are male with the exception of Paula Ward, Director of Donor Relations. Unfortunately, a departmental restructuring eliminated her position, but as of this date in 2009 Judy Williams now works on the administrative level in World Missions.

In general, the pattern I saw on the website in 2006 was very clear: men served in leadership positions and women were 'Administrative Assistants' (a term for secretaries) on the whole. The sexist divide was solidified by the fact that I did not find any men occupying the role of Administrative Assistant or Receptionist. However,

---

[10] Spencer, 'Solemn Assembly', p. 10.

the actual state of affairs at the headquarters or RDC is not fully represented on the website.

To gather a little history, I turned to my mother, LaDonna Scott.[11] Scott recalls that Margaret Muse Oden started the Archives Department in the early 80s and that Doris Moore also served as Archivist. Both women served under the General Superintendent. In addition, Charlene West served under the Executive Director of Evangelism as the Hispanic Director. Finally, Barbara James served as Co-Director of the WIN program (intercessory prayer ministry) under the direction of the General Superintendent. However, all of the above positions have been hired, not elected, positions; and Paula, Margaret, and Doris were not at the RDC very long. Barbara James served for eight years and then retired when Bishop Underwood left office.

Scott also recalls that both Doris and Shirley Spencer started at the RDC as secretaries. Shirley started as Frank Tunstall's secretary when he was editor of *The Advocate*. When he left, Bishop Williams appointed Shirley as the Executive Editor; but she has never been on the RDC payroll because she is paid by LifeSprings, although the Publications Department is under the General Superintendent. Shirley has been at the RDC around 34 years, and she has served the longest of any woman at the RDC on the administrative level.

However, just as with any other entity, the IPHC is not stagnant in its vision or practice. Scott also wrote the 2005 conference spoke to the issue of women and as a result a woman was appointed to serve on each of the general boards. Unfortunately, these boards were not part of the General Board of Administration (GBA). The GBA is the highest administrative board in the denomination and is composed of approximately sixty members representing the general offices (elected officials), conference superintendents, institutional administrators/presidents, pastoral, lay, Hispanic, African American, and women representatives from across the denomination. Following the general conference in 2005, there were five women on the GBA. Two of these women were elected to serve and three were appointed. The two elected were Trish Weedn, elected to the General Executive Board, and Jewelle Stewart, elected by the Women's

<hr>

[11] For this section, I relied upon LaDonna Scott, 'Personal Correspondence' (July, 2009).

Ministries Convention as the general executive director. Three other women were appointed to serve: a lay representative, a pastoral representative, and Shirley Spencer as editor of the IPHC *Experience*.

More recently, at the 2009 general conference, the people voted for a total restructuring of the denomination on the general and conference levels. On the general level, the General Executive Board of thirteen members was reduced to four elected individuals serving as the Executive Council for the Council of Bishops. The former GBA is now called the Council of Bishops; and only the Executive Council and the conference superintendents make up the Council of Bishops, thus reducing by approximately half the membership of the highest governing body between general conferences. There are presently no women serving on the Council of Bishops. A new board was formed called the General Ministries Cabinet, which does include two or three women in administration from the RDC (now called Global Ministries Center); however, this is not a legislative body. The general boards did follow the 2005 general conference and appointed a woman to each of the general boards.

The IPHC's history reflects efforts made to help bring women into leadership positions. One example is a short piece written by Former Bishop James Leggett called 'Affirming Women in Ministry'. In it, he writes, 'Though the Pentecostal Holiness Church has always encouraged women in ministry, the numbers of women in ministry today do not reflect this. The church must be more open to women in every phase of leadership. Women helped launch the church in the first century. Their ministry is crucial to an effective church in the 21st century'.[12]

Therefore, although a problem with gender-based prejudice persists in the IPHC, the purpose of this book is not to bemoan that status but to explore the lives and experiences of women preachers in Oklahoma in the context of their place and time in history with a recognition that sexism was still an obstacle for them, even inside of a religious tradition that has given a voice to women preachers. It

---

[12] James D. Leggett, 'Affirming Women in Ministry', *IssacharFile* 3.3 (March 1999), p. 2.

is also to call for more inclusion of women in the administrative offices of the denomination.[13]

'Challenge It and It Will Change'

In April of 2006, thousands of Pentecostals converged on Azusa Street in Los Angeles, California. I was among them. I will never forget feeling so small in that sea of people, but neither will I ever forget the pride I felt in being a part of such an enormous, vital religious force. If only a fraction of Pentecostals were represented at that celebration, then I felt the reality of our numbers was great indeed. In fact, Dr. Cho reported 'over forty thousand people from 103 countries' converged at the L.A. Convention Center and Sports Complex, among a variety of venues since many speakers were scheduled to speak in the mere four days set aside for the celebration, April 25-29.[14] Furthermore, although historian Vinson Synan once estimated a conservative two hundred million Pentecostal believers, Dr. Cho's website quotes The World Pentecostal Fellowship, who 'announced that there are an estimated 600 million Pentecostal and Charismatic adherents in the world today: 165 million in Asia; 158 million in South America; 150 million in Africa; 83 million in North America; 34 million in Europe; and 4,600,000 in Oceania'.[15] Clearly, the global influence of Pentecostalism is enormous today, and although the IPHC is just one denomination among them and although I am just one believer within that denomination, what can be learned through my idiosyncratic experience of it can in some ways be an extrapolation of what it is about this movement that makes it so engaging for so many people in so many countries today.

On a Tuesday evening, out of all of the services being held, I chose to hear the well-known Pentecostal preacher Paula White. In January of that same year The Christian Post had named her as the

---

[13] At the 2010 Appalachian Quadrennial Conference, Rev. Wanda Myers was elected to Conference Executive Council as a 'Member at Large'. She is the first woman ever elected to this position.

[14] David Cho Evangelistic Mission, 'An Exuberant Spiritual Experience: The Azusa Street Centennial', <http://www.davidcho.com/neweng/Main_News.asp?nsel=&no=60> (3 July 2009).

[15] Again, the numbers of Pentecostals vary based on the definitions of Pentecostalism.

thirty-seventh most influential Christian in America, above the Pope who was named forty-fourth. President Bush was named sixth and, to no one's surprise, African-American preacher T. D. Jakes was named first.[16]

People were being bussed to a variety of locations. My mother and I had to stand in line for the bus to take us to hear Paula White. Once there, we had to stand in a line that wound for as far as I could see. Paula White preached in Aimee Semple McPherson's Angelus Temple. I felt strange sitting in a building I had only seen in pictures, but I was then enraptured by the service that began with a procession of people carrying flags from all of the different major countries of the world. This exercise emphasized the international status of the Pentecostal world.[17] Perhaps in its instantiation, the abolishment of racism was limited to closing the divide between black and white, but today it is so much more than that.

The worship service emphasized the veneration of God and Christ through the gifts of the Holy Spirit (that is, through speaking in tongues), though there was no singular message and interpretation as sometimes occurs during Pentecostal services. However, Paula White occasionally spoke in tongues during her sermon, and it was clear that the experience of greater spiritual power that is gained through the baptism of the Holy Spirit was still a vital part of the practice of Pentecostalism today.

White openly spoke against racial and gender-related prejudices ('Prejudice is to judge out of a narrow frame of mind'), and she challenged listeners with the question: 'What were you born to do?' 'To exist is a waste of days', she said. 'Some people say the most important dates are the day you were born and the day you die. But the most important dates are the day you were born and the day you figure out why'. Her inspiring sermon left me with a message I emphasize in much of my work: 'Challenge it and it will change'.

As the service progressed, the Holy Spirit inhabited the place. To my left, a young black man worshipped loudly and boldly. To my right, my mother wept and quietly spoke in tongues. I surveyed the

---

[16] 'Fifty Most Influential Christians in America', *Online Edition of the Christian Post* (January 2006), <http://www.thechurchreport.com> (18 August 2006).

[17] At the IPHC's South Carolina Centennial celebrated this June of 2010, the international theme was also reflected in flags from around the world which decorated the main building.

people in the crowded auditorium, noting the diversity in terms of age, race, wealth. I saw diversity in worship as well. Some were of the quieter sort as I am; some were flamboyant. I felt God had brought me here to see the twenty-first century community of believers in order to see our unity. Denominational boundaries sometimes divide, but to have so many come together and worship in peace together was astounding.

When I completed my dissertation in 2007, I was left with the feeling that I had contributed to a community that extended far beyond the International Pentecostal Holiness Church, a growing, global community that thrives on acceptance, equality, and the love of Christ as the Holy Spirit confirms, directs, and empowers his people to do so within a sense of unity. The autobiographies and transcribed interviews in this book reveal that these ideals are not always perfectly practiced or supported, however, but the present state of the IPHC and its influence on the nature of Pentecostalism at large leaves us with some satisfaction as well as great hope for the future.

APPENDIX

The Ministry of Ruth Moore[1]

[Baker begins with general observations about her mother, Ruth Moore.]

My mother grew up in Texas. They had a large family and were very poor. They chopped cotton for a living and moved from farm to farm. I don't know if they owned land; they may have just been tenants. They were not religious people; they did not attend church.

When my mother was around seventeen years of age, she attended a brush arbor meeting in Woodville, Oklahoma, located near the Texas line. She received salvation during this meeting. I don't know who held the revival, but she was the only one of the family who got saved. She had nine brothers and sisters and then her parents. She committed all to the Lord and was determined to serve Him even though her family did not.

Soon after her conversion she began preaching. She traveled with Lee Hargis and his wife to hold revival meetings in Oklahoma. She evangelized two women first. Both of their first names were Anna. She said, 'I don't know what I said. I knew nothing, not being raised in church or anything, but I guess I said something!' Then, she went to Bible College.

I remember mother telling me once, she was humming, 'I will go where you want me to go', and her mother said, 'Oh, Ruth, you don't mean that' and she said, 'Yes, I do'.

She had to leave home but she went to live with her grandfather in southern Texas. And he was the one who paid for her to go to Bible school at King's College in Kingfisher, Oklahoma. Of course, that was affiliated with the PH church.

She met Ed Moore while attending King's College. By that time she must have been nineteen or twenty. They were married Septem-

---

[1] This appendix is an interview with Wanda Baker, the daughter of the deceased Rev. Ruth Moore. The interview was conduced in the fall of 2004.

ber 14, 1929, while she was in her second year of college at the age of twenty-one.

Her parents fully expected her to come back home. They never expected, in fact, her father gave her first Bible because she was so developed in her faith and so determined, but they just couldn't accept that she wasn't coming back. And, it was probably because of her age that they just couldn't accept that. Yet, all of her family came to totally depend on her for prayer. By going to be with them and praying for them, she led almost every one of them to the Lord.

When was your mother born?

She was born on May 20, 1908. She joined the Oklahoma Conference in 1931. My dad was Pentecostal Holiness too. He got saved at a little PH church in Mountain View. My parents lived in Enid, Oklahoma, where my father was employed at Long Bell Lumber Company. All five of us children were born there. Brother Rex, your grandfather, was our pastor. I think Brother Finkenbinder was the first pastor that I vaguely remember.

Mother's first pastorate was a church in Drummond, Oklahoma. She pastored this church until her first child was born in 1931. After they started their family, she felt they were her priority and did not pastor again until 1945.

She was faithful to her church in Enid and held a few revivals. In 1943, we moved to Oklahoma City. My father was employed at the Douglas Aircraft plant, and we attended the First Pentecostal Holiness Church. My mother was preaching a revival at this church when World War II ended.

In August of 1945, she was asked to pastor the Central Pentecostal Holiness Church in south Oklahoma City. My mother was the minister and my father was the administrator. They were a good team. During this pastorate my father oversaw the construction of a new church building and parsonage and two other houses, which were sold to help finance the church construction. He was an excellent builder and helped in the construction of several churches in the Oklahoma City area. They were at the Central Church five years. Also, under their leadership, a church in Moore, Oklahoma, and one in Del City were established.

Their last pastorate was the Trinity Pentecostal Holiness Church in Oklahoma City where they stayed for twenty-five years. After my mother died in 1968, my father continued to pastor until 1984. He said later that he had felt 'called' when he was younger, but he felt like he had to make a living for his family. He started preaching when they went to Trinity, but that was not until around '58 or '60. My mom did all the preaching up until that time, and my dad took care of the business part and the board meetings. It was what my mom wanted because he had expertise in that. It worked well.

Mother and Daddy loved the Pentecostal Holiness Church. They loved to go to the general conventions. Daddy was a delegate almost every time. He went as a lay delegate for many years. In 1958, my mother was sent as a delegate to the youth convention in Franklin Springs, Georgia. My husband and I went with her. After she arrived, she felt she was too old to be a youth delegate so she asked me to attend the sessions with her.

Mrs. Baker wanted to respond specifically to the questions I had previously mailed to her asking if her mother had ever had any difficulties as a woman preacher, just because she was a woman.

She never had a problem with recognition or with needing a role in the church. She did have some challenges because not everybody accepted women preachers. I remember a problem one time when they were building the church on Central and we were worshipping in a tent. They erected the tent right on the ground, and it was a cold winter. The wind went through it although we had an old stove in the middle for heat. We had a revival with Brother Rex in the tent. Well, there was a Church of Christ group who decided to challenge the fact that mother was a preacher because they didn't think she should be. They came and, of course, mother opened the service as the pastor of the church, and they came right down on the front row and sat down. The good thing is that Brother Rex was right there ready for them, and he just talked to them and took care of the situation. We felt like the Lord worked that out because she didn't have a confrontation with them. Brother Rex knew just what to say. But that's the only confrontation, face to face, that I know that she had.

She was loved by her people. She was not flamboyant. She was very shy, very feminine. She never took on the demeanor of a lot of women that adopted sort of a masculine demeanor. Mother was very shy and was not a conversationalist. She was a wonderful listener. I would call her, and we would be on the phone for a long time and she would say very little. She would not say a lot, but she would say enough to let me know she understood. And, as I said, my family, we loved her dearly.

I asked her what 'number' her mother was out of the ten siblings that survived.
She was the fifth one born out of ten children. Her mother had some twins that were stillborn, and then there was another child that didn't live very long. So, there were actually thirteen.

We were talking about my father being poor, and I told Mrs. Baker a funny story about my parents' early days of marriage which reminded her of the following story:
My father had a terrible time 'catching' mother. Every time he thought he had her, she would write him and say she'd changed her mind. So, my father had found another woman and was going to ask her to marry him one weekend. My mother called him long distance and told him that she was going to be holding a revival with somebody and thought he would just like to know. So, he knew that she had changed her mind again.

I asked her if she remembered when her mother got filled with the Holy Spirit.
She was not married yet, so she had to have been seventeen to twenty-one years of age. I think she must have been eighteen or nineteen years old, and she went to a camp meeting. One of these 'Annas' was there and another lady by the name of Killebrew. She was filled with the Holy Spirit. She was laying in the Spirit all night until the morning. In the morning—it was 5:00 or 6:00 in the morning and they were getting ready to start because they were going to have a sunrise service, as they did in those days. When they were starting the service, she was filled with the Holy Spirit. And those two women had stayed with her all night; they would tell about it too. I remember Mrs. Killebrew telling about it. My mother was sanctified. She was a great believer in sanctification. In the *Pentecostal Message* she has a sermon on sanctification. But that experience did so much for her. And I think that experience and determination

helped her keep her commitment to the Lord. Brother Rex's sermon on holiness helped too.

Mrs. Baker wanted to respond to a question I had mailed before the interview where I asked about whether her mother considered being a preacher a job.

She did not regard her work as a job, but as a 'calling'. She followed her calling because she felt so strongly in her heart about it. What she preached, she lived and she believed. We were pleased to have a lot of, you know, Brother King, Brother Muse, and a lot of leaders of the church in our home when we were growing up. And mother always felt her position was that she was more comfortable when men were in charge. She felt that women should not usurp authority over men. She was willing to serve and do what she was called to do, but she really felt that men should have leadership in the church.

My mother was very concerned with world events. She voted; she always voted. It really wasn't just being submissive, that she felt she must be submissive; it was what she preferred. For her, it provided comfort for her. Because she was a leader, she was a minister; but she was not an administrator. Even though she enjoyed preaching, she was not an administrator. That's why she was comfortable in that way.

I asked her if she thought of 'submission' more like 'cooperation'.

Well, I know there were a lot of women, especially in the early days of Pentecost, that truly felt depressed; and I think that maybe they resented that. But my mother, even though my dad was the head of the family, they talked everything over. If my mother didn't agree, she didn't say so in front of us; but when she had the opportunity with just the two of them, they would talk. They just wanted to do whatever it took to be true Christians.

My dad was not raised in church. His mother died when he was very young. I remember one time my father decided the girls needed to wear cotton stockings because that was what they did in those days. So, mother prayed and she finally asked him about not doing it. And he said, 'Okay'. She didn't always agree with everything dad did, but she waited until the right time to discuss it with him. So, that was such a wonderful example for us.

When I was talking to my sister, we couldn't remember them ever having a fight. We knew that they had their discussions, but they didn't blow up when we were around. Mother was submissive; but if it was something that she felt that she needed to talk to dad about, she did.

Also, I remember one time when I was young, a preacher came to our house because he was holding revival at our church. We were having lunch and I said, 'Remember, Mother, you are going to cut my hair tonight after church'. Mother always trimmed my hair for me, and the preacher said, 'You don't cut your daughter's hair!' And mother said, 'Well, yes, I do!' But you must remember back then that was a big controversy to cut your hair.

One time when she called and we were talking about it, she said, 'Wanda, I try to look at things this way. Is it going to hurt their experience with the Lord? If it's not, then you can't take everything from them. You try to weigh it that way'. And, that helped me a lot. They were strict, but the things that they felt we could do, they let us do so that we would not have bitter feelings. And none of us do. Even though there were things that we didn't do, it never hurt me. None of that ever hurt me. It helped me. Even though I don't live up to all those things, it helped me to make better choices in my Christian life. Mother and Daddy were just wonderful examples to us in every way.

They did not have a 'you're going to do it because I said so' attitude. They had a kinder, gentler attitude. They tried to make life enjoyable for us. I don't ever remember being unhappy. I was always happy. Even though we didn't really have a lot at all, I was always happy. They didn't go to the extreme. Even though Mother didn't cut her hair, she cut mine. And she gave me perms and all of that. But I did have to wear long sleeves and long socks. But I felt like because they really prayed about things, I think the Lord gave them wisdom; and they did the best job they could.

That is such a great testimony.

BIBLIOGRAPHY

Ackley, Heather Ann and Annette McCabe, 'Dynamics of Ministry Training and Ministry Opportunities for Charismatic Women: Socio-historical Perspective of Wesleyan, Pentecostal, and Holiness Women in Ministry in the Nineteenth and Twentieth-Century US', *Cyberjournal for Pentecostal-Charismatic Research* (February 2006), <http://www.pctii.org/cyberj/cyberj15/Ackley_McCabe.html>.

Alexander, Estrelda, 'Introduction', *Philip's Daughters: Women in Pentecostal-Charismatic Leadership* (Eugene, OR: Pickwick Publications, 2009), pp. 1-18.

Anderson, Allan, *An Introduction to Pentecostalism* (Cambridge: Cambridge University Press, 2007).

Backhaus, Gary and John Murungi, *Earth Ways: Framing Geographical Meanings* (Lanham, MD: Lexington Books, 2004).

Bakhtin, M.M., *The Dialogic Imagination* (ed. Michael Holquist; trans. Caryl Emerson and Michael Holquist; Austin: University of Texas Press, 1990).

Barfoot, Charles H. and Gerald T. Sheppard, 'Prophetic vs. Priestly Religion: The Changing Role of Women Clergy in Classical Pentecostal Churches', *Review of Religious Research* 22.1 (September 1980), pp. 2-17.

Benvenuti, Sheri R., 'Pentecostal Women in Ministry: Where Do We Go from Here?' *Cyberjournal for Pentecostal-Charismatic Research* 1 (January 1997), <http://www.pctii.org/cyberj/cyberj1/ben.html>.

Berlin, James A., 'Contemporary Composition: The Major Pedagogical Theories', *College English* 44 (Dec. 1982), pp. 765-77 (repr. in Victor Villanueva, Jr. [ed.], *Cross-Talk in Comp Theory: A Reader* [Urbana, IL: NCTE, 1997], pp. 1-19).

Bizzell, Patricia and Bruce Herzberg (eds.), 'Richard Whately', *The Rhetorical Tradition: Readings from Classical Times to the Present* (Boston: Bedford/St. Martin's, 1990), pp. 828-30.

Brekus, Catherine A., *Strangers and Pilgrims: Female Preaching in America, 1740-1845* (Chapel Hill: University of North Carolina Press, 1998).

Brooks, Ronald Clark, 'Historicizing Critiques of Procedural Knowledge: Richard Weaver, Maxine Hairston, and Post-Process Theory', *College Composition and Communication* 61.1 (2009), pp. 90-106.

Burke, Kenneth, *The Rhetoric of Religion: Studies in Logology* (Berkeley: University of California Press, 1970).

Campbell, Joseph, *The Pentecostal Holiness Church, 1898-1948* (Franklin Springs, GA: The Publishing House of the Pentecostal Holiness Church, 1951).

Cherwitz, Richard and James Hikins, 'Rhetorical Perspectivism', in John Louis Lucaites, Celeste Michelle Condit, and Sally Caudill (eds.), *Contemporary Rhetorical Theory: A Reader* (London: The Guilford Press: 1999), pp. 176-93.

'Christians for Biblical Equality' (2010), <http://www.cbeinternational.org>.

Corder, Jim, 'Argument as Emergence, Rhetoric as Love', *Rhetoric Review* 4.1 (Sept. 1985), pp. 16-32.

—'Varieties of Ethical Argument, with Some Account of the Significance of 'Ethos in the Teaching of Composition' in Richard E. Young and Yameng Liu (eds.), *Landmark Essays on Rhetorical Invention in Writing* (Davis, CA: Hermagoras Press, 1994), pp. 99-134.

Curtis, Grace Hope, *Pioneer Woman for Christ: The Life and Ministry of Grace Hope Curtis* (Tulsa, OK: Johnnie Hope & Associates, 1978).

Cox, Harvey, *Fire From Heaven: The Rise of Pentecostal Spirituality and the Reshaping of Religion in the Twenty-first Century* (Cambridge, MA: Da Capo Press, 1995).

David Cho Evangelistic Mission, 'An Exuberant Spiritual Experience: The Azusa Street Centennial', <http://www.davidcho.com/neweng/Main_News.asp?nsel=&no=60> (3 July 2009).

Dirksen, Carolyn, 'Let Your Women Keep Silence', in Donald N. Bowdle (ed.), *The Promise and the Power* (Cleveland, TN: Pathway Press, 1980), pp. 165-96.

Enos, Theresa, '"An Eternal Golden Braid": Rhetor as Audience, Audience as Rhetor', in Gesa Kirsch and Duane H. Roen (eds.), *A Sense of Audience in Written Communication* (Newbury Park, CA: Sage, 1990), pp. 99-114.

Faigley, Lester, *Fragments of Rationality: Postmodernity and the Subject of Composition* (Pittsburgh, PA: University of Pittsburgh Press, 1992).

'Fifty Most Influential Christians in America', *Online Edition of the Christian Post* (January 2006), <http://www.thechurchreport.com> (18 August 2006).

Fulkerson, Mary McClintock, 'Joyful Speaking for God: Pentecostal Women's Performances', *Changing the Subject* (Minneapolis: Fortress Press, 1994), pp. 239-98.

Graff, Richard and Michael Leff, 'Revisionist Historiography and Rhetorical Tradition(s)', in Richard Graff, Arthur Walzer, and Janet Atwill (eds.), *The Viability of the Rhetorical Tradition* (Albany, NY: SUNY, 2005), pp. 11-30.

Grady, J. Lee, *Twenty-Five Tough Questions About Women and the Church* (Lake Mary, FL: Charisma House, 2003).

Hargis, Lucy, unpublished letter (on file in Bethany OK: IPHC Archives, 1975), pp. 1-35.

Holmes, Pamela, 'The "Place" of Women in Pentecostal/Charismatic Ministry since the Azusa Street Revival', in Harold D. Hunter and Cecil M. Robeck, Jr. (eds.), *The Azusa Street Revival and Its Legacy* (Cleveland, TN: Pathway Press, 2006), pp. 297-316.

Horowitz, David, 'Why an Academic Bill of Rights is Necessary', *Students for Academic Freedom* (15 March 2005), <http://www.studentsforacademicfreedom.org/news/997/OHohiotestimony031505.html>.

Hyatt, Eddie, *The Azusa Street Revival: The Holy Spirit in America, 100 Years, Special Centennial Edition* (Lake Mary, FL: Strang Communications, 2006).

Hyatt, Susan, 'Spirit-Filled Women', in Vinson Synan (ed.), *The Century of the Holy Spirit: 100 Years of Pentecostal and Charismatic Renewal 1901-2001* (Nashville: Thomas Nelson, 2001), pp. 233-64.

'International Pentecostal Holiness Church', <http://www.iphc.org>.

Jernigan, C.B., *Pioneer Days of the Holiness Movement in the Southwest* (repr. by Charles Edwin Jones, 2002; Kansas City, MO: Pentecostal Nazarene Publishing House, 1919).

Johns, Cheryl Bridges, 'Pentecostal Spirituality and the Conscientization of Women', in Harold D. Hunter and Peter D. Hocken (eds.), *All Together in One Place: Theological Papers from the Brighton Conference on World Evangelization* (JPTSup 4; Sheffield: Sheffield Academic Press, 1991), pp. 153-65.

Kennedy, George, *New Testament Interpretation Through Rhetorical Criticism* (Chapel Hill: University of North Carolina Press, 1984).

LaBerge, Agnes Ozman, *What God Hath Wrought* (repr., New York: Garland, 1985).

Lawless, Elaine J., *Handmaidens of the Lord: Pentecostal Women Preachers and Traditional Religion* (Philadelphia: University of Pennsylvania Press, 1988).

LeFevre, Karen Burke, *Invention as a Social Act* (Carbondale: Southern Illinois University Press, 1987).

Leggett, James D., 'Affirming Women in Ministry', *IssacharFile* 3.3 (March 1999), p. 2.

Lucaites, John Louis, Celeste Michelle Condit, and Sally Caudill (eds.), *Contemporary Rhetorical Theory: A Reader* (London: The Guilford Press, 1999).

May, James M., 'Ethos and Ciceronian Oratory', *Trials of Character: The Eloquence of Ciceronian Ethos* (Chapel Hill: University of North Carolina Press, 1998), pp. 1-12.

Mercy Seat Films, 'They Closed Our Schools' (2003), <http://www.mercyseat films.com/aboutfilm.html>.

Miller, Thomas P., 'Reinventing Rhetorical Traditions', in Theresa Enos (ed.), *Learning From the Histories of Rhetoric: Essays in Honor of Winifred B. Horner* (Carbondale: Southern Illinois University Press, 1993), pp. 26-41.

Momaday, N. Scott, 'The Delight Song of Tsoai-talee', *The Poetry Foundation*, <http://www.poetryfoundation.org/archive/poem.html?id=175895>.

Noren, Carol Marie, *Woman in the Pulpit* (Nashville: Abingdon Press, 1991).

Ong, Walter J., 'The Writer's Audience Is Always a Fiction', *PMLA* 90 (January 1975), pp. 9-21.

Oden, Margaret Muse, *Steps to the Sun* (Franklin Springs, GA: The Publishing House of The Pentecostal Holiness Church, 1955).

Palmer, Phoebe, 'Tongue of Fire on the Daughters of the Lord', in Patricia Bizzell and Bruce Herzberg (ed.), *The Rhetorical Tradition: Readings from Classical Times to the Present* (Boston: Bedford/St. Martin's, 2000), pp. 1100-113.

Paul, Harold, *From Printer's Devil to Bishop* (Franklin Springs, GA: Advocate Press, 1976).

Peterson, Susan, 'Patient, Useful Servants: Women Missionaries in Indian Territory', in Melvena K. Thurman (ed.), *Women in Oklahoma: A Century of Change.* (Oklahoma City: Oklahoma Historical Society, 1982), pp. 106-14.

'Quaker Mary Dyer', <http://www.mass.gov >.

Reuther, Rosemary Radford, *Sexism and God-Talk: Toward a Feminist Theology* (Boston: Beacon Press, 1983).

Rex, Robert, *I Was Compelled by Love: People Called Me 'Mr. Evangelism'* (Franklin Springs, GA: Advocate, 1982).

Roebuck, David, 'Pentecostalism at the End of the Twentieth Century: From Poverty, Promise, and Passion to Prosperity, Power, and Place', in Corrie E. Norman and Don S. Armentrout (eds.), *Religion in the Contemporary South: Changes, Continuities, and Contexts* (Knoxville: University of Tennessee Press, 2005), pp. 53-74.

Scanzoni, Letha Dawson and Susan Setta, 'Women in Evangelical, Holiness, and Pentecostal Traditions,' in Rosemary Radford Ruether and Rosemary Skinner Keller (eds.), *Women and Religion in America: 1900-1968* (San Francisco: Harper and Row, 1986), pp. 223-65.

Scott, LaDonna, 'Biography of Bishop James Leggett' (Unpublished interview, June 2006).

Smith, Craig R., *The Quest for Charisma: Christianity and Persuasion* (Westport, CT: Praeger, 2000).

Spencer, Shirley, 'Solemn Assembly Marks New Beginning for IPHC', *International Pentecostal Holiness Advocate* 80.4 (November 1996), pp. 4-13.

Synan, Vinson, *The Century of the Holy Spirit: 100 Years of Pentecostal and Charismatic Renewal 1901-2001* (Nashville: Thomas Nelson, 2001).

—*The Old-Time Power: A History of the Pentecostal Holiness Church* (Franklin Springs, GA: Advocate Press, 1973).

Vander Lei, Elizabeth and Lauren Fitzgerald. 'What in God's Name? Administering the Conflicts of Religious Beliefs in Writing Programs', *WPA Writing Program Administration: Journal of the Council of Writing Program Administrators* 31.1-2 (Fall-Winter 2007), pp. 185-95.

Wallace, David L., 'Alternative Rhetoric and Morality: Writing from the Margins', *College Composition and Communication* 61.2 (2009), pp. 18-39.

Weaver, Richard, 'Language is Sermonic', *The Rhetorical Tradition: Readings From Classical Times to the Present* (Boston: Bedford/St. Martins, 2001), pp. 1351-360.

Welch, Kristen D., 'Appendix F: Personal Letter, Lennie Cordie Gilcrease Rex, Date Unknown', *Oklahoma Preachers, Pioneers, and Pentecostals: An Analysis of the Elements of Collective and Individual Ethos within the Selected Writings of Women Preachers of the International Pentecostal Holiness Church* (PhD Dissertation, University of Arizona, 2007).

—'Post-1960s Pentecostalism and the Promise of a Future for Pentecostal Holiness Women Preachers', *Cyberjournal for Pentecostal-Charismatic Research* 16 (January 2007), <http://www.pctii.org/cyberj/cyberj16/welch.html>.

West, Charlene, *Life is a Great Adventure: Discovering Truth in the Journey of Faith* (Mustang, OK: Tate Publishing, 2007).

White, Richard, *It's Your Misfortune and None of My Own: A New History of the American West* (Norman: University of Oklahoma Press, 1993).

White, Paula, untitled sermon, *Azusa Street Centennial: Paula White* DVD (Divide, CO: Lampstand Studios, 2006).

York, Dan, *The Life Events of Dan and Dollie York* (repr., Oklahoma City: Charles Edwin Jones, 2002).

INDEX OF BIBLICAL REFERENCES

Old Testament

New Testament

INDEX OF AUTHORS

INDEX OF NAMES

Other Books from CPT Press

R. Hollis Gause, *Living in the Spirit: The Way of Salvation* (2009). ISBN 9780981965109

Kenneth J. Archer, *A Pentecostal Hermeneutic: Spirit, Scripture and Community* (2009). ISBN 9780981965116

Larry McQueen, *Joel and the Spirit: The Cry of a Prophetic Hermeneutic* (2009). ISBN 9780981965123

Lee Roy Martin, *Introduction to Biblical Hebrew* (2009). ISBN 9780981965154

Lee Roy Martin, *Answer Key to Introduction to Biblical Hebrew* (2009). ISBN 9780981965161

Lee Roy Martin, *Workbook for Introduction to Biblical Hebrew* (2010). ISBN 9780981965185

Martin William Mittelstadt, *Reading Luke–Acts in the Pentecostal Tradition* (2010). ISBN 9780981965178

Roger Stronstad, *The Prophethood of All Believers* (2010). ISBN 9780981965130

Steven Jack Land, *Pentecostal Spirituality: A Passion for the Kingdom* (2010). ISBN 9780981965147

www.ingramcontent.com/pod-product-compliance
Lightning Source LLC
Chambersburg PA
CBHW072352090426
42741CB00012B/3017